Nation Building
Is the Heart of Religion and the Leap

From Zoroaster to Plato, Moses
and Paul To Nation Building

MOSES, LUTHER, **NAPOLEON AND PERICLES TRIED AND LOCKE AND JEFFERSON PULLED IT OFF.** LOCKE'S DREAM FELL TO COLONIALISM AND TWO WORLD WARS OVER COLONIES. JEFFERSON'S U.S.A. WAS LOST TO NATIONALISMS IN THE WORLD WARS. *THE 'PROJECT NATION' CONTINUES AS BROTHERS KENNEDY LIKE TO PUT IT.* ROME'S GAIS BROTHERS EARLIER SO DREAMED THE GOOD DREAM INCLUDES WOMEN, **PEOPLE OF COLOR AND THE POOR IN THE NATION PROJECT.**

John R. Fielden

authorHOUSE®

AuthorHouse™
1663 Liberty Drive
Bloomington, IN 47403
www.authorhouse.com
Phone: 1 (800) 839-8640

Published by AuthorHouse 09/08/2016

ISBN: 978-1-5246-2263-3 (sc)
ISBN: 978-1-5246-2261-9 (hc)
ISBN: 978-1-5246-2262-6 (e)

Library of Congress Control Number: 2016912547

Print information available on the last page.

CONTENTS

BOOK TITLE----MOVEMENT POLITICS AND RELIGION WHILE BEING EVANGELICAL ABOUT NATION BUILDING THAT PLATO AND ABRAHAM STARTED--NIEBUHR-RORTY-CHARDIN AND COMPLEXITY CONSCIOUSNESS ARE CONSIDERED IN NATION BUILDING BEYOND LOCAL TRIBALISMS

1. Reinhold Niebuhr's neo-orthodoxy as nation building with movement sensitivity in the Protestant movement is a set of propositions and not just love babble. In West Texas the wind pumps the water and the cows cut wood but water is over pumped and wind now best produces electricity. Texas Tech in Lubbock needs more movement history, philosophy and co-ops to move citizenship education beyond football and technics.

2. Myth for Niebuhr is not just special widening of percepts as Jung, Whitehead and Buddha but is our complex conscious mind holding complex interests in a peace and consequences dialectic system which we may call democracy----the goal being to create a culture of efficiency balanced by sufficiency in creating quality education for all children. Early courses in philosophy is a human right to counter the culture biases of family and local tribal truth systems.

3. Niebuhr's critical realism focuses on univocal creation and our later human creativity, minus privileged access to archetypes that reveal God. Niebuhrian myths do not reveal God behind metaphor as is so with Spong, Crossan and Borg, but criticizes the real issues of nation building with Plato and Abraham.

4. Alain de Botton sees efficient mechanical causation as important but sufficiency causes need adding as in Hume's emotive-sympathy education concerning deep culture movements in history----technology is not enough. Richard Rorty's reading of 'Uncle Tom's Cabin' is better than Texas preachers, love babble and apolitical science math curriculums. De Botton's 'agape café' claims we can move deeper to a sufficient society over mechanical efficiency and sports education.

5. What is sufficient education for the young? Mark Twain's America and J.W. Krutch's "Great Chain of Life" can help. Krutch focuses on animal heroics along with our claim to truth's beyond science, math and religious sayings. Rorty, like de Tocqueville, values conversational dialectics to help aggregate public policies---this means education focused on real possibilities with John Dewey. Rorty, as Jesus, uses irony in stating complex goals that are value added involving new space and time tested propositions.

6. De Botton and Rorty are for common-sense dealing with gravity, birth control pills, atoms, guns and wealth re-distribution---clearly the soils, moderate climate and water were not created by capitalism. Capitalists did plow up the west creating the 'dust bowl' after killing the buffalo and Comanche Indians.

7. Common sense means conversation with neighbors to formulate public policy for land, water, energy, education, courts and elections. Niebuhr was for deep suspicion of pride and ego in utopian politics concerning sect, class, gender, tribe, race and national security---his suspicion was not so extreme as Camus in matters of slippery slope propositions inside of democratic time-framed elections. FDR. focused on HEW – housing education and welfare as the Social Gospel for basic needs met. Even Richard Nixon proposed an economic floor under families.

8. Professor Thomas Noble once taught at Texas Tech---he is now at Notre Dame---his focus on great world movements form Athens to the present could help us avoid epileptic fits of salvation---William James saw that these fits of salvation are not all bad as they come at a time when the young realize, on their own, that the ego-culture has left out too much. Youth culture fantasia can be partly cured

by serious historical courses on world movements that are not found in the movies.

9. Common sense may need help from 'wall propaganda' as Epicurus claimed, as well as in churches and the de Botton agape café. The Japanese use art and steady signs to remind them that their islands are in the earthquake zone and the other quakes that have come to the islands include various Buddhist invaders with a developed Confucian ego from "Mother China" as well as from Western colonial hegemon states.

10. Our religious problem is nation building—this is so because we need both nation building and institutions like the church-unchurch to critique the nation when it gets too certain that it is a chosen nation---holding such a complex dual consciousness (nation and church-unchurch critic of the state) is uniquely possible for conscious human beings. The Cold War (1950 to 2000) demonstrated our crisis when anxious capitalists saw the chance to use religion as national ideology. This madness allowed the nation to retribalize as a whole culture dissolving all internal doubts in behalf of a limitless Pentagon budget.

John Fielden

MY BOOK IS READY TO DIGITIZE, SLIGHTLY EDIT AND PRINT---THE BOOK TITLE ANNOUNCES A BROAD THESIS THAT RELIGION IS ABOUT NATION BUILDING---SOME ESSAYS ARGUE WITH MODERNS SUCH AS FAREED ZAKARIA---WHO WAS TRANSPLANTED TO COMPLEX NATION BUILDING IN AMERICA FROM COMPLEX TRIBALISM IN INDIA.

1. Arguments may repeat in contexts---each essay has a title that is hopefully worked into the body of the essay. The essay titles may be altered or merely left to announce content.
2. A page for complex definitional issues may include Reinhold Niebuhr's view of univocal-creation and conflicts of interest within the created---another view of the univocal creation is Plato's Demiurgos that predicts a dual causative within the created world.
3. Protestantism will variously be defined as protesting theocracy and military states.
4. The Christian, Paul, will be discussed along with Jesus, as proposing nation building in a dual polity (church and state) context where 'church' includes secular propositions such as the American New Deal and the Ford Foundations Hutchins Center in Santa Barbara discussing various studies of democratic institutions.
5. Great dramas in some essay topics include the world naval empires of the Spanish and English and the Cold War of the twentieth century featuring the United States being united in fear of Communism.

6. The Industrial Revolution in the cotton mills of 19th century England involves protesting churches such as the Quakers, Methodists, Presbyterians, Unitarians and the unique English Parliament.

7. The drama of German unity, up to the present crisis of a European Union and NATO, is the picture of modern powerful tribes becoming a nation with a Parliament serving to give political parties responsible demonstration-time-in-power. Bonhoeffer and Niebuhr met at Union Theological School in N.Y to discuss complex nation building in the U.S and Germany––with the extremes of race and sect treated as long besetting problems for nation building in both cases.

8. Rome's pretense to be a nation and also a theocracy is given some space via Augustine and Constantine.

John R. Fielden
480-894-6745
2004 E. Vaughn St.
Tempe, Az. 85283

CHOICES—CHOICES—STAYING OFF THE STREET AND OUT OF JAIL IS NOT THAT SIMPLE----CHOOSING A TRIBE OVER A NATION HAS TEMPTED SOME OF US---TRIBES HAVE CHIEFS WHO WATCH THE BORDERS AT A PRICE TO ALL OF US.

1. Pericles tried to unify Athens by culture sharing and joining the Delian League. Tribes defend borders but lack the interactive process of citizens within borders. Persian and Syrian tribes threatened Athens and Jerusalem. Egypt was not tribal until often invaded across the Nile.

2. Horse tribals, in the "central Asian dynamic", endlessly threatened the Chinese, Russians and Indians---the Chinese tried a wall, the Russians depended on the Cossacks and the Buddhists left India as the Islamics attacked their symbolized god-persons. India tried pluralism and today has a big bomb. German tribes and the Vikings were too much for Rome. Tribal chiefs do the border with fear-itself as a powerful psychological tool.

3. English and Spanish navies altered the tribals, but added religious missions and colonial theocracy in acting as super tribes over borders. The Industrial Revolution in England created tribes and dissident protesting churches joined Parliament for the Ten Hours Act of 1847. Caesar was wary of German tribes and the Scots and came home over the Rubicon to mess over the Roman Republic and set up military-religious leaders. Constantine dealt with the tribes from the inside via the trinity-mind-set and added bread and circus to hold the interim.

4. Nothing is free but things are cheaper in the tornado zone---people do move around and need safe travel. Churches are tax free but need to be maintained and cooled-heated. At some point in life, choosing the next meal may be more urgent than promises of a next life. De-sexing the family reveals emotions are basically important over sex. The police need over-sight and to be paid as does the military, lawyers, courts, teachers, librarians. Social security and the minimum of housing, education and welfare must be paid for. Specialty medicine in remote areas can be a crisis. Even Methodists have choices beyond grace and the choir.

5. The United States has a long border with a nation that lost some of its water supply to us---deserts are not always fun. Europe has a long and very loose border with the desert tribes and their internal wars now threaten Europe. Russia has trouble forgetting past invasions from the west as does China. Choices--choices. Once the church is heated and cooled some will want new furniture---staying out of jail and off the streets is complicated.

SOURCE OF RELIGION---NATION BUILDING---GREEK AND HEBREW DIASPORA TO ROME AND OVER THE ALPS TO HEGELS NATION SPIRIT

1. The Greeks and Hebrews went into a great and long diaspora as Sparta, Persia and Alexander crushed Athens and Jerusalem. Moses and Abraham were into abstract lists of behaviors and holy places with a theocratic order. Zeus faded in the whirl of nation building and Yahweh made a best try and moved west to Italy for a new start. Augustine and Constantine tried a new unity---a mystical trinity for Constantine and a vague political duality of church and state for Augustine that would slowly evolve over a thousand years---from 400 to 1400 A.D.

2. The Greek revival was delayed by Hellenization or the psychology of stoic and epicurean adjustment. Plotinus favored a great unity of all reality coming out of Gods body and Jesus and Paul proposed a dual polity that Challenged the Roman military state. The Greek revival we call the Italian-Greek Renaissance.

3. Ways to unify the German tribes was not obvious---monastics sought to soften the tribals and in time the French Carolingians and the Spanish drove Islam back into Africa. India's pluralist religion could not stop the Islamics and Indian Buddhists retreated over the Alps to China.

4. The French were isolated after their attempt to move the Pope to Avignon. Rome and the Pope moved in with the Spanish navy and the remains of monarchist princes in the eastern agricultural feudal groups intermarried with the Spanish crown. Imperial

pretension and nationalism joined Rome and Spain to colonial empire building. If Italy was not ready to be a nation it could become a part of Spain's and Habsburg's naval empire. At last, Napoleon had France join Europe and set off Hegel's great spirit of German unity---later Bismarck and Luther tried again. German unity was delayed by Luther and Catholic theocracy and the delay became an opening for Nazi gangs.

5. England's navy and Tudor's state church felt secure enough for protest which we may call latitudinarianism of protest. The protesting church and Parliament passed the Ten Hours Act in 1847 to protect wage workers from the cotton factory lords in the English midlands---Yorkshire etc.

6. Unity in America came with chattel slavery in the Constitution (our original sin) and moving the Indians to western deserts--- Reservations would presumably protect the Indians from manifest destiny or Gods holy experiment. Small free farms might help the French peasants and might help drive the Spanish from Florida, Louisiana, California and Texas. The American Constitution doesn't work because it is a set of republics only pretending to unity---states rights groups and a so-called Supreme Court has held some sense of unity but the Court is not in the Constitution and can be a tool of strategy for rising corporate interests that were absent in 1800. A Darwinist reading of the Constitution started as great American corporations entered the race for colonial empires in the late 19th century. The Court and Adam Smith joined to protect free enterprise from regulations that might produce a social gospel state such as the New Deal that faced the Court in the 1930s.

7. Russia's long war against Islamic theocracy was often been ignored as Russians remembered the colonialism and unifying mistakes of the west under Napoleon and Hitler. Russia is a cold place and the wheat that grows in the Ukraine has never fit inside a defined nation. Russian now has oil and a long memory. The U.S. has gotten involved with Islamic oil with the Saudi Sunni sect and has only lately awakened to theocratic oil. Russian oil and Islamic oil have not been solved by positive thinking in America. Wind

and sun have been neglected and general lack of intellect about historical forces has left the U.S. puzzled about oil alliances.

8. The Internet has opened politics to criminals and terrorists----selfies on the phone are like positive thinking---they are distractive to a society that needs a deeper sense of the mess that we have created----the public schools distract or else worship science gadgets----some of which are helping organize the theocrats. Democracy is hard to produce---we need a variety of media and not Fox News that is simply corporate propaganda. The schools teach history as boring dates and places and no sense of interpretation.

9. History is complex----Unitarians in England kept a clear view of the social crisis in the industrial midlands but colonialism finally turned England into troubles----the romantics movement turned Unitarians in America to scientism---god or nature as the optimistics like Emerson remanced frontier nature and spoke to God via the over-soul or over-thought self.

10. History is the history of philosophy and not just the history of military leaders and particular sects of religion. Protest is broader than Protestantism---and is an entry to the free intellect that entertains some uncertainty---even the young deserve to know how little we know. A small town on Caddo Lake in East Texas can help save the oil patch and old slave south from its self---it is Uncertain, Texas.

EARLY PAGE LISTS ALTERNATIVE BOOK TITLES

1. Religion did not merely fall out of the sky. (My first book was about land, water, wind and cow stuff to replaces wood.)
2. Zoroaster's pragmatism---is legacy judgments at the Chinvat Bridge of the Decider. Legacy judgment of American presidents-- Teddy Roosevelt-Wilson-Reagan are all under judgment at the American Bridge of the Deciders.
3. Democratic grids---Sun and Wind politics versus corporate coal and oil theocrats.
4. In Tuscany, up the Arno River---a horse race to Siena for nation building--is the long human project.
5. Galileo measured 'balls' in space and time in Pisa---Machiavelli moved actual things in space-time for the first time in Florence-- this makes Plato and Socrates proud.
6. The Protestant Revolution can not and should not be completed--a Niebuhrist view.
7. Hutchin's Center for the study of Democratic Institutions--is a church and state study of democratic institutions. Hutchins would add Parliament as the real trinity in practical politics.
8. Dual polity in Jesus, Paul and Augustine accepts an imperfect world or a pragmatism that makes a difference. Constantine would make the world better via a mental trinity council, bread and circus and two military capital cities. Marcus Borg and a choir think love is a Subaru and can create reality by language ---and take a metaphor to lunch.
9. Zoroaster's pragmatism at the Bridge of the Decider accepts an imperfect world with a pragmatism that makes a difference.

10. Reinhold Niebuhr and Plato's 'realism' seeks a balance of human interests and not a 'realism' of Kissinger and Nixon---or a balance of military tribal groups.

11. Kierkegaard can ask if a leap to a third strategic politics or co-op-ist strategy can cure Darwinist economics extremes?

12. Augustine and Paul favored an extended time for love and justice eschaton debates over German tribalism.

13. Schweitzer favored an extended eschaton time over colonialist time---his piano, a hospital and a life-world philosophy on the way to the Congo.

14. A Manichean dualism (a Zoro sect) is in effect a monism-effect or world disloyalty as Whitehead would say.

15. Mistaking Islam for another sect is a basic mistake---saying nation building is evil is not mere sectism. Islam is an anti-ecumen religious viewpoint-or theocracy for clerics.

16. Lord Maynard Keynes would balance out economic crises for Germany and the world with something like the negative income tax to favor family income floors---Nixon was better than Watergate flaws---his negative income tax got him fired by the followers of Adam Smith.

17. Leaving justice and love to social science is love as a Subaru in the labyrinth of noise.

18. Plato's ideas and forms would turn atomic facts into testable values in the space and time of Florence and the new republic.

John R. Fielden

PROBABLE AND SUGGESTIVE MOVES
OF MY ESSAYS INTO A BOOK

1. Book asides: --- may go at end or start of the book.
    --- dictionary devotions
    --- Ivy League preparations
    --- picture of Monkey Wrench for my father's project
    --- Fareed Zakaria a response
    --- Las Cruces and Prescott adventures.

2. The main thrust of my book is the failure of Greek and Jewish groups to start nations or commons midst warring tribes and their subsequent moves west to Italy-Europe in a Great Diaspora. Rome's long pretense at empire and nation, failed to unify with German tribes, while Constantine held back the Arabs and Russia helped the Greeks to some security via Kiev and Moscow as the new Jerusalem for Eastern Christians.

3. St. Paul and St. Augustine proposed dual polity authority systems and John Locke and Jefferson, at last, gave it a try.

4. Zoroaster's legacy politics failed and the extreme world-denying Zoro gnostic sects moved west to France as Cathars and as Manicheans at Carthage.

5. Greek philosophy revived in the Italian Renaissance, with time and place propositionals for a new Athenian Republic.

6. The long Protestant Revolution north of the Alps continues to protest against theocracy and single party politics---the Industrial Revolution pushed the protest to a Ten Hours Act by Parliament in 1847. with protesting churches and the state proposing the Ten Hours Act to help the new wage-slave factory workers.

7. In the Christian middle ages, epistemology and ontology were revived as theories of reality more complex than previous concerns about essences and named differences---Greek dialectic arguments challenged the logo-centrics where the premise and conclusions were the same in tautological self references. Logo-centrics Abelard and Ockham, like moderns Borg and Nelson (Beatitudes Center in Phoenix), were challenged by Anselm, Aquinas and Eckhart for real propositions about real problems. Baruch Spinosa tried to help Descartes out of his puzzle of two realities---God and physics by combining the two in a romantic new lens that revealed both God or nature in the same linguistic logo-centric move---this allowed science to be a mental scientism or psychology that synthesizes small things back to the dark space of univocal cosmic beginnings.

8. American Great Awakenings in religion and politics allowed Reinhold Niebuhr and C.W. Mills to enter the Cold War dialogues with America as a virtual empire midst two world wars---Eisenhower saw it as the new American military-industrial-complex.

9. Modern post-moderns like Walter Bruggemann wants the modern pulpit to do what he saw Yahweh trying to do as nation building over tribals---negotiating with powers that be in the name of victims of hegemonic colonialism for white men only. Bruggemann wants to introduce post modern thinkers----post Descartes and Spinosa to renegotiate powers that be such as gender, race, sect, tribe and class. In this adventure he needs the help of French and German thinkers---Heidegger, Sartre, Camus, Ponty and Husserl. He mentions Rorty, Habermas, Lyatard and Khun as new thinkers beyond the logo-centrics and those comfortable with the vague language of God or nature knowing in R.W. Emerson and friends---whose over-soul sounds like private help from deity sneaked back into all conversations. Rorty was sure that such would stop modern conversations. Habermas would agree, but hopes to keep some subjectivity in the premises via the German language of Schweitzer---world loyalty or life-world spirit.

10. Existential Europeans such as Heidegger, Sartre, Ponty and Camus hope to keep a responsible-self-in-the-making as our project central.

11. The oil-coal and sun-wind wars continue with oil and coal on the side of theocrats and oligarchs The crisis of no natural border leaves NATO in trouble with Russia and the Ukraine food basket ----Russia has oil but also endless war on her southern borders. Russian history has some bitterness with the West, but the West is no longer the English navy and England's desperate search for cotton and colonies. May NATO survive!

12. Lyndon Johnson lost the old south and East Texas but tried to save the German Hill Country and the Nemitz Museum to the pacific war (Fredericksburg) in the west-southwest of Texas. Johnson favored the poor Mexicans in the Hill Country, but wanted the Germans to feel welcome there too---they had come in by sea and build homes and churches of stone---there were no trees and Bob Dylan had said everyone has to get stoned sometime.

13. South by southwest includes Austin and Tucson---Ed. Abbey and the Monkey Wrench, J.W. Krutch and heroic desert animals---they also worried that tourism would steal the water and turn the west into a winter home for the Scottsdale rich. Others would agree---Molly Ivins, Robert Solomon etc.---the South by Southwest might save the desert from conservatives who would waste it on lawns swimming pools and golf. Desert Solitaire could be a start on being nice to animals for engineers and a new complexity consciousness.

14. The Mt. St. Michel conversation or 'Walk' in France, deals with modern complexity and anxiety for a politician begging for corporate money, a poet (Naruda) hiding from the C.I.A that kills left thinker-dreamers and the science lady who wants to be clear and distinct with Descartes but finds science in the mists of corporate power and self-referenced truth claims dumping wastes in rivers and oceans. The mystical retreat for monks at St. Michel is unable to find an essence beneath all the greedy interests.

15. The Big Four of Texas are suggestive---the Amherst Co-op Hospital, C.W. Mills reveals the Cold War as a new conservative religion----Molly Ivins retreats to Austin as the Texas media is oil-coal, hats and boots ---Shelby Knox thinks women's centers are needed---Plato would agree---urban jobs have changed and

the womens-can-do, as Plato had hoped---alter birth patterns and politics of war.

16. Nixon and Dulles in the Cold War created the Republican Party---Nixon was clever (tricky Dick) in suggesting we are all Keynesians now and ought to help poor families, Bill Clinton was clever in triangle politics---the modern King David ---he and Dole would free Kosevo from the Serbs and keep Russia angry as did Wilson at the end of World War One. The mushy epistemology of Spinosa's God or nature in love with love will get you an off-road Subaru, scientism as a faith, and better scopes for Galileo and the off-road researchers.

17. My book need not sell---it is just a monkey wrench and not a money wrench---it is not essential but is a walk minus big hats and boots.

DEFINE RELIGION AS A LEAP TO A COMMONS OR ROUSSEAU'S GENERAL-WILL PAST THE TRIBALS

1. The problem for atheists and theocrats is they don't know what religion is or has been about. Nation building is about practical negotiations, using Greek dialectics, to define public policies in defined spaces.
2. Nation building stops some wars between democratic nations. Small states like Athens and Jerusalem do not work well and operate as tribes---always with fear at every border.
3. U.S. separate states as republics are too small and in crises they join the military industrial complex as in the Cold War of the 20th century.
4. Religion is at war with theocratic tribes or caliphate-like assemblies of clerics who make civil laws for the tribes.
5. The general will is altered by experience. The U.S. New Deal has been time tested but is never complete. Medicare specialists are not available in remote and small towns. Food stamps are hard to verify for those without addresses. Cities may declare areas self-policing for those living without homes---some live in tents as see Las Cruces N.M. The risk of living in such areas may be balanced by a sense of community even for the most poor.
6. The 'general will' means medical doctors may become U.S. employees and not free enterprise operators. The Amherst Co-op Hospital was owned by farmers and hired doctors without permission of the American Medical Association––the farmers exercised a general will or monkey-wrench-gang versus a money-wrench-gang. The general will may turn libraries and other public spaces into political and educational spaces for public debate.

7. Churches are tax free space and may become DVD Universities in their class spaces as another way to declass society. Churches may challenge Locke's courts by providing money and space for defense lawyers.

8. Nation building will mean military budgets are to be debated---monopoly media may favor military sequestered budgets---the American South has been military-minded and an easy target for the military industrial complex.

9. Socrates and Plato identified the military industrial as complex special interests. Various Jewish prophets identified military interests and fear-itself as part of military politics. Churches may use co-ops to create new media that counters the military industrial complex. Churches need not own the co-ops but by strategic political action over time may alter the harsh effects of free enterprise while defending free enterprise.

10. Zoroaster proposed strategic politics in his legacy realism---if politicians sin they can be tried in public opinion at the Chinvat Bridge of the Decider. George W. Bush was the decider---the public now judges him for the Iraq war.

11. Buddhism has atheistic aspects and has not helped build the Chinese nation. After flight from Islamic terrorists into India the Buddhists have been slow to build China into a nation and the Marxists have used the vacuum to create another China. In India, Brahman religion has been class-based but the times they are a changing---Robert Oppenheimer saw a new world of the Gita at Whitesands New Mexico. He saw Vishnu, Krsna and Shiva, the classless gods, now rising in India. The Hindu Party now has the A-bomb and is creating an India that is not completely at risk from Islamic tribes, but the work of Vishnu, Shiva and Krsna is barely underway.

12. Buddhist went to China to avoid war with theocratic Islam and now still has two boats---a great boat is speculative and next worldly and the small boat is left to priests and prayer to keep values and general will in negotiation. Tao and Zen Buddha as existential and individual choices complicates the general will in being-for-others.

13. Marxist China now takes U.S. jobs as Republicans drove out U.S. Unions––this made China rich in making things---tax free to Walmart stores. As the U.S. takes back the jobs and Unions. China is now in crisis to make things for the Chinese masses.

14. Confucian China is part of their general-will-culture as family centered, and may be seen as part of the way to block Islam's move into the islands south of China---tight Chinese families face off Islam in Indonesia and the southern Philippines.

15. World Religious studies should not be turned over to those without back grounds in political theory and history of philosophy. Questions in context depend on the adequacy of contexts---the intellectual side of religious studies should not be left to news reporters.

FOREVER POST-MODERN----CAN WE BRING THE GREEK PHILOSOPHERS BACK TO SAVE US ALL?

1. The Greek way was dialectic in considering fair contracts, peace values that limits the military tribal who live by 'fear itself' at every border and a search for new potentials for complex cooperation inside a defined political time and space that we call nations. Thanks to Socrates, Plato and Aristotle. Paul was a Greek Christian in his dual polity church and state premise. The Greeks were both into the ideal and real, but in geography Alexander crushed all tribes and states into an empire that became Rome. Empires are not tribes nor nations, but are Caliphates that hope to rule via mystical claims to God and the creation of a psychology for stoic and epicurean mind games plus bread and circus distractions order that could last a thousand years.

2. The Hebrews, via Moses and Abraham, tried to be post-tribal and leap to a nation-commons, but like Athens they were too small and attached to such tight rituals and the language of holy places that they were a set-up for Alexander and Rome. Moving west seemed wise---the Hebrews in a great Diaspora and the Greeks to Italy to attempt a great renaissance of their own in the late medieval centuries. Italy turned out to be a poor place to unify a nation and powerful mystic pulls to a great oneness spread with Plotinus from 300 BC to 1300 AD---here stoic and epicurean Hellenism replaced the Greeks. Plotinus has some of Plato's original univocal cosmics drive to have all of reality be part of God's body---but this leaves out Greek dialectics and actual nation building.

3. Rome was beset with various moves to the west such as the Zoro sects like Manicheanism that settled across from Rome in

Carthage. Manichean dualism in Carthage was an actual monism of world-denial and Augustine and Constantine gave that only a moment before moving to another unity view---such as the trinity for Constantine and a verbal unity of church and state for Augustine.

4. In Florence and Venice two Greek republics reset contract theory and values over security or military madness---Machiavelli made various unity or nation building attempts, using the humanistic psychology of the stoics and epicureans, but stronger interests kept hopes from happening---the rich de Medici arts family, the Pope and his militarist son (the Borgias), the German tribals who came south for Christmas when the Rhine froze over yearly and the Spanish loved every port in Italy for their rising navy.

5. The French also saw Italy as theirs---the Carolingians in the 7th and 8th century drove the Isamics from western France and over the Pyrenees into Spain---this set the stage for later inquisition against the Cathar Manicheans in south of France. French kings were little Popes and in time held the popes captive in Avignon. On Christmas day 800 AD Charlemagne went over the Alps and was crowned Roman Emperor by a Pope that felt intimidated. Charlemagne's march left the Eastern or Constantine Catholics wary of the western Christians.

6. Meanwhile back in Italy two new republics---in Florence and Venice slowly lost the sea to Islam and Rome turned west to a new empire with the Spanish navy creating a colonial empire along with Spanish inter marriages to the Habsburgs of Austro-Hungary.

7. North of the Alps the Germans had no navy but the agricultural feudal princes allowed Luther to protest and create a nationism that was a virtual theocracy that did not fit the larger protests that grew in England protected by the English navy. The Dutch and English navies created a second set of Christian nations and a world naval war with Spain.

8. Moving west was complex and some protestants feared Rome so much that they sought a pure start in the American wilderness. Puritans did not trust the Tudor states slow latitudinarian view that might allow Paul's vision of a dual authority politics or church and

state that came to be the Lockean Parliament and in the Industrial Revolution and turned the church and state into democratic policy making ---the Ten Hours Act or 1847 was a great example of Pauline politics in the cotton mills. The cotton mills used slave cotton but the Protesting churches got the 10 Hours act to secure worker rights in the new era or wage slavery. Meanwhile others in England would use the navy to build a colonial empire---as another slavery and leave Parliament weak until the 20th century.

9. John Locke has some sense of Greek philosophy in his Deism and dialectic processes but he also has his own theory of property as congealed labor----this ignores the crisis of unfair contracts and courts that may represent opportunity for the propertyless. In the cotton mill towns the propertyless did need more than a Ten Hours Act and a right to vote. Property theorist drifted into colonialism and turned some churches into land grab theology or saving native peoples souls while taking their cotton lands. English colonialism may be seen as causing two world wars and turning England into a 51st state in the new American empire––(1920 to 1950)

10. In America, the Puritan's crisis in nation building ran into the new sin of chattel slavery and moving the Indians west to dry Reservation to live off and with the buffalo. What was pure was hard to find in America---the Unitarians here were not like those in the English Industrial crisis---romantics could move west with Emerson and seek both God or nature in a manifest (as Spinosans---or another Plotinus allness). Could Kant's good-will unify the anxious new republic on a wild frontier that even lacked feudal unifying rules. A unique new empire of space unified by a constitution with slavery and republican states rights still held in a mind set moving west----is a troubling uniueness.

11. Dutch and English navies and soul saving theology came to disaster in two world wars---some still called it civilization building as did some Catholics for the Spanish empire. German tribes, at last, moved into unities---Hegel's national world spirit, moved as the owl Minerva at dusk, for a new home for the night---the French did not know how to use the coal and iron of the Ruhr

border––their art was elsewhere. Three American Republican presidents in the 1920s left France to return to the arts and pretend a unity of sorts---the Comteans suggested they create a religion just for France that would be Positive. Positive thinking also came to the U.S. for Eisenhower and the anti-Communist Republicans tried positive thinking. Eisenhower was not ready to join the military industrial complex that claimed to win the world wars. Radical nationalism and anti-Communism ideology together with a Comtean positivism as an ideology seemed to be a new reality. C.W. Mills and Reinhold Niebuhr saw the theocratic side of the new empire as a corporate mind game not unlike Rome's bread and circus. Big time sports, especially football in big stadia, was as distracting as Hollywood movies and was creating a new social culture. Mills saw the media being used to create happy robots in the American empire. Drop kick me Jesus through the goal-post-of life was positive enough even for small towns when dominoes was not enough.

12. Back to the Greeks or forward to the Greeks---was or is the culture cave too deep to be challenged?

DICTIONARY DEVOTIONS

1. Heuristics--- are thoughts held as possible but in such doubt as to be a kind of reality---we may call this 'high theory' to loosen the locked in math minds and the overly urgent believers.

2. History is a long history of Abraham's failure to deal with Sodom and Gomorrah and seek a Socratic contract for justice.

3. The Pope, at last, says don't breed like rabbits---sending priests over the Alps was an early experiment in sexual religion---now we need to move on dot-org.

4. John Crossan seeks a just-contract with Yahweh and a synthesis with love as a Subaru of logic in the labyrinth of tautology.

5. The Ten Hours Act by Parliament (1847) was a church-state-church product at last.

6. Cotton thread is a Methodist fiber---but the cotton mills cried for help and not just a choir.

7. England avoided a nasty French Revolt by becoming a cotton-kingdom even without local cotton----desperation for more cotton---Gandhi did knit his own small pants and the English went home without their nasty little certainties.

8. The cotton ships also created wage-slaves in the Yorkshires---the English enclosures movement replaced sheep with wage-slaves in the factory towns.

9. Methodists need a foreign policy other than Phoenix rising out of the desert.

10. God was a householder for Nixon's negative Keynesian income tax---it also got Nixon fired by his party.

11. Marcus Borg loved Methodism---it is just a fight for love or a Subaru of love chasing love----metaphor is for those with little historical imagination.

12. Plato and Anselm would create values out of atomic facts---we may call this a second creation for univocalists.

13. Socrates without a contract is just a Socrates Café.

14. Scientisms love the new Spinosan lens of God or nature---love is a Subaru---say it slowly.

15. The largest choir wins if the pulpit is empty and all are gone to Ghost Ranch to rethink the whole project of protest with protest content.

16. Ed Abbey's monkey wrench is protestantism for the red canyons.

17. Joseph Krutch says desert animals have the fighting soul of protest that Darwin could not find in the islands.

18. Schweitzer with piano and life-world in hand challenged colonialism and the eschaton of theological history.---with no imminent eschaton a small one here.

19. The Jesus Seminar is a Subaru of love that Heidegger thought to embolden with a towardsness epistemology.

20. Heidegger's towardness is an episte of modesty in Niebuhr's world of no clear endings.

21. Would David Hume be a Methodidist of sorts ---he liked generalized values over lists of facts---he could have lived in graceland with Abelard and Wesley.

22. Locke's reasonable Christianity assumed a dialectic with three Greek stages---with justice left in the middle and some uncertainty as a healthy negativity.

23. Kant's good-will and free-will fills Hobbes's and science labs with anxiety and the courts with lawyers.

24. The Tudor navy gave the Popes and Spain a tutorial in nation building.

25. Uncertainty is a conversation with Richard Rorty and Habermas---a conversation society.

26. Complexity consciousness scares my southern relatives who are unconscious.

27. Bill Clinton and Bob Dole drove the Slavic Russians out of Kosevo and the principle of sovereignty out of fashion, so the Bushies could play with restructuring the old English colonies.

28. Sex education in Lubbock, Provo and Mecca keeps the absolutist test alive.

29. Sherman leveled Atlanta so it can become the black capital of Georgia replacing Carterville Georgia.

30. The Chinvat Bridge of the Decider was pragmatic but requires a varied media and reading public---Gore Vidal doubted that we have such a society.

31. We have replaced the English empire with Teddy Roosevelts and Wilson's world of the Admiral Zumwalt and the military industrial complex.

32. We now have NATO to replace colonialism and the mystic trinity psychers.

33. Sun and wind politics versus coal and oil theocracy is important --- oil theocracy is not just another religious sect, but it acts like one.

34. Tuscany, up the Arno River to Siena and Florence, brought back the dream of the Athens republic---a good debate about whether cloth merchants could build fortress homes that are higher than city hall was a space and time matter not left to Galileo in Pisa.

35. The Protestant Revolution can not and should not be completed---the Niebuhrs and Plato were willing to eternalize the uncertain.

36. Robert Hutchin's Ford-Center-for-the-study-of-democratic-institution suggests the church-state dynamic is not finished---the dialectic in Santa Barbara now includes ways to desalt the water as well as re-think the Greeks in America.

37. Galileo measured balls falling in Pisa while Machiavelli sought a pragmatic way to unify Italy in actual political space and time that is unscientific but feels good.

38. In Florence, the de Medici made art out of money and the Borgia Popes and Savanarola made my southern natives proud by burning their hot pants.

39. Kierkegaard needed a third leap or co-op to cure the Darwinist enterprisers and German nationists.

40. Nixon's spying on the Watergate was fun and not as serious as saying we are all Keynesians now----Barry Goldwater could not take that kind of heuristic theorizing and fired the thief.

41. Take ice cream directly form a baby and human nature has written a scream into the script----a sense of justice is immediate-----an innate sense of justice is suggested.

42. Spiro Agnew, vice president for Nixon, attacked the 'nattering nabobs of negativity' in response to Herbert Marcuse's claim that Americans are in danger of becoming 'nattering yabobs of positive thinking' or the narrowing of the mind to fit the business model to everyday thinking. President Coolidge had said the business of America is business.

43. Natanyahu has said God gave the west bank and the Jordan River to Israel---what God did as a yahu we may never know

44. John Locke is said to be a good empiricist but his theory of rights seems no more certain than Kant's claim for 'good will' planted in our pyche.

45. Theocracy is not another religious cult but is anti-nationalism and anti-democracy in the sense that nations are premised on a commons tax base and a commons spending of taxes base.

46. A Caliphate is a holy-city in the sense that clerics live there. A Caliphate is a declaration of war against tribes and nations outside the symbolized area.

47. Values are symbolized bundles of atomic facts that can be united as a possibility and held in purpose driven consciousness.

48. Don't imminentize the eschaton means stop trying to build a final utopia on earth.

49. Via negativity means a new cosmology may arise negating this one.

50. A dual polity defines church and state as a theoretical 'one-in-Parliament-made-laws'. The term 'secular' is a synthesis activity inside and outside of a particular Parliament.

51. Islam is against nations, as distractions from deity, but their Caliphates act as a form of nationalism around declared holy places.

52. Santayana was for animal spirits but he saw the long overlapping cultures of England creating a culture of co-operation that is another spirit.

53. Was Nixon's crime, not Watergate, but his Keynesian proposal to balance social incomes in response to economic cycles that Adam Smith had ignored---so his claim 'I am not a criminal' in the ordinary sense of criminality is correct.

THE PROTESTING CHURCH

1. The pulpit is important as a comforter and promoter of minor charities and replaces carpets. The comforting purpose of the pulpit is to protest the impersonal forces of commerce and mere efficiency of larger cities and project a mild sense of 'we' without over doing sect history.
2. The social gospel may support a specific political party or not, but in off the pulpit classes only.
3. Police and prison oversight and end of death sentences is important church work.
4. Critical education concerning nationalism and flagism---see Reinhold Niebuhr here.
5. H.E.W. church specifics include---single payer health plan, six years free 'higher' education and social security--- age and condition related.
6. Sex education---the public schools fail here---churches can step up.
7. Energy grids for individual homes---sun and wind replacing coal and oil---churches all have roofs and the sun and wind are wholly owned god sources for householders.
8. The Courts-ACLU invited as guests and money for defense lawyers is important.
9. Union guest speakers by invitation.
10. Churches can enter into long term strategic co-ops to alter media ownership and build community centers.
11. All citizens vote via national identity cards----to include sheriffs and mayors.
12. Foreign policy discussions---there are no holy places---only holy peoples.

13. Critical of single book education whether the Bible or Francis Bacon's idols of science. There is a difference between science education and science propaganda.

14. Bacon's idols include theatre---Rousseau noted the distractions in Versailles, the market idols---market competition is a U.S. idol, idols of the cave—–culture caves lock in minds too early, idols of tribe---the 'we-are-the-holy-people-view' prevents nations doing commons building.

15. Galileo's two book strategy is useful if one of the 'books' includes the Greek philosophers along with Paul's 'other authority politics' and Lockean Parliaments. Churches are part of Galilio's book two. Universities are selling degrees and not truth---some generalizations are true----complex co-operation involves universal health care, auto safety, air cleaning efforts---the churches can make electricity and help create DVD University---churches can house a few defense lawyers. Galileo did need to visit Florence to complete his eduction.

LANGUAGE ACTION THEORY---THE PERFORMING PULPIT--YODER AND HAUERWAS TILLICH RUSSELL AND THE PEACE CHURCH---CAN MODERNS HUSSERL AND SARTRE RESPOND?--AMERICAN HISTORY HIGH EPISTE AND ONTOS THEORY

1. In the 1630s new-light-theory of Jon Edwards started to do what Locke and the English were doing by asking about unfair first position contracts with Socrates---the Puritans facing a wild frontier did need new light.

2. In the 1730s Emerson's over-soul sought a change in the pulpit favoring more sermons on god or nature (Spinosan) and less on salvational sermons---Emerson hoped the over-soul would give the Puritans something to be pure about in moving west to an open frontier. The over-soul appears to be mystical and Kantian in claiming noumenal truth over mere phenomenal truth.

3. By 1790 Walter Rauchenbush at his Hells Kitchen New York Church faced a new frontier of unemployed masses pouring into the city and the need for labor unions---American corporations were becoming more powerful than local state and city governments.

4. By the 1920s the open frontier was over and a crisis in urban America started to look like Rome with bread and circus---sports, mass media entertainment and wage slavery hanging on after chattel slavery had been defeated---the after effects of chattel slavery also an on-going crisis in the 20th century. Reinhold Niebuhr and C.W. Mills wanted to expose the circus and return America to a more modest world view and even a new view of sin. Niebuhr saw

sin as extreme power temptations in the arena of human interests---i.e. gender, race, class, tribe and sect. Moderating extremes within democratic politics seemed a crisis with the Supreme Court taking Darwinian views of public policy and the U.S Military Industrial Complex boasting it represented god or nature for a new world order and virtually owning several state governments that perform like monarchies in Orwell's 1984 novel---it truly was novel and questionably American.

5. Existentialists refocused on the individual and Heidegger-Husserl and Sartre sought actual projects where human responsible choices could be tested. Nation building may be seen as the central problem of religion and America and Western Europe was in a crisis over peace and war ----did the churches help or did they act like tribes (sects) and fall into sermons mostly about falling clover and salvation? Did peace church have a place in live politics in America? Did the Churches join the new corporate world order? At Duke University Yoder and Hauerwas favored the peace church and presumed right of churches to help propose and do public policy. Rick Roderick lectured on deep change---Duke was still tobacco and coal rich. Unions needed national help but the South feared unions would include blacks---the National Relations Labor Board might organize the unorganized. In New Mexico worker committees have sought help from the NLRB. Several U.S. states try to deny unions any status.

6. The Republican Party favors trade and says robots and small government can out produce foreign slave states---Reagan Republicans were anxious to be rid of Unions. The Old South states have tried to make unions illegal. Niebuhr would say the crisis is deeper than peace church---the U.S. Constitution is not a united state except in war and as an empire we are always at war since the Puritans came ashore. Nation building with Unions was the way before Reagan.

7. We cant read the Bible apart from conditions as Tillich imagines---Wittgenstein at last gave up on language as did Russell but Whitehead added process games (as Jung and Chardin) where god

of nature do 'Spinosan speak' in the grace church. Kant's good will noumena is itself a kind of language.

8. Bruggemann says Yahweh negotiated for a nation in behalf of David, even knowing David had a bad moral record. Stoics and psychologists since Plotinus (300 BC-1300 AD) have sought a great oneness---signs and shadows-archetypes was God for Joe Campbell and Bill Moyers on TV. Rorty left the language phils in Virginia for literature of Uncle Toms Cabin at Stanford---later Rorty was pushed into nationalism versus Islamic killers with money trails---he would torture them for sources.

9. Emerson in the USA was a Unitarian pantheist romantic, less focused on modern evil of factory work than were the Methodist-Unitarians in the cotton mills---new wage slavery could be solved by moving west---Unitarians in the Yorkshires saw Jesus joining unions. Emerson at Harvard played with blowing clover in sermons--- his god or nature for pulpit sermons to replace salvation ceremonies. He toyed with Owens like utopias for his back yard but rejected Brookfarm---and he ignored chattel slavery until Whitman and Thoreau got his attention.

10. In England the Fielden-Methodist-Unitarians opposed agriculture subsidies that ran up the price of corn and they opposed the Tudor Poor Laws that used harsh methods on those who left the factories. The factory towns were an early version of 1984 and Animal Farm. The new factory world crisis was soon added to by distractive media, sport, movies and a new feudalism.

11. Yoder, Borg and Hauverwas favored a peace church but there was no peace if the churches sang America the beautiful as war budgets go up and up. America and Europe need to be unified nations and the leap to a democratic polity.

WELCOME TO A YAVAPAI HILLS
DINNER IN PRESCOTT MISS KITTI

For two years we lived midst super rich homes at 'The Ranch' in Prescott Az.---these homes came from unearned money of homes sold in foggy valley California. Prescott is an authentic nut-house area somewhat like Phoenix and unlike Tucson. In Prescott two maverick Unitarian groups dislike each other and started two churches---the one down town was appropriately located in the Odd Fellows Hall. In Yavapai Hills I knew a Methodist guru woman who could organize a Christian birthday for Moses. I wrote a note suggesting a little Valentine party for the Prescott asylum (Odd Fellows) group that we favored. This guru had run a positively single group at Crossroads Methodist Church in Phoenix. She was married to an engineer she had met at a dance near the church. He was a great dancer and she organized him despite his engineering past.

Hi Miss Kitti---we met her often downtown Prescott for breakfast---yall might be interested in a Yavapai dinner party ($ 30.00 for two) by our friend the super party Methodist guru in Yavapai Hills. As Democrats we have decided on the French policy of governance---policy first and then scrutinize the scrutables. Kitti claims she had sex with Ken Starr and has decided on her own to cover that up---partly as a conspiracy against him for having a minus personality and a small thinga. Instead of following Nietzsche's path of tautological and self-referenced critique of reason we are reading Heidegger, Deridda and Foucault. Why not seek analogies to reason in the everyday practice of communitarian propositional truths, normative rightness and subjective truthfulness with Richard Rorty and friends----all this authentically enmeshed with each other. See you at the party.

■ ■

We lived two years in Las Cruces, New Mex. Here we met a couple from the Julliard School of music---in Las Cruses he played with the Big Band of the Rio Grande. They were very Jewish and were advised by the Julliards to seek Unitarians in Texas and the west---tolerance has some limits. He was proud that he had marched some Nazis off into a forest in WW 2 and let them know he was Jewish. He was a safely advocate for safe cars before the Denver Law School hired him to council lawyers on how to avoid trial courts. He did not fit well with Unitarians so we started a domino group at several member homes. He would preach slightly at these meetings and tell various old Jewish jokes about escaping from the Russian military crusades---usually there was no place to go but over a cliff-----the next life was never quite clear. I tried to give the Rio Grande some larger meaning with dominoes---LBJ claimed the United States had a domino policy that included keeping the Communists out of the delta ---he lifted his shirt to show a long scar which was like the delta. Keeping the United States out of Texas, we might start with the Texas domino game called 'forty two'. If the game caught hold we might reclaim the area up to the Rio Grande. Forty Two parties kept us together. My Jewish friend thought he saw signs of a Christian conspiracy even among Unitarians. The Unitarian minister's last name was Christian.

THE AMHERST CO-OP HOSPITAL

There are no laws of nature, except perhaps gravity. Now we know that "dark matter" has less clear laws of relationships than Newton imagined. David Hume would add human sympathies or sentiments to our human constructs such as the Amherst Co-op Hospital.

The American Medical Association defended medicine practiced as a 'fee for a service', but Doctor McDaniels took his chances and became our co-op doctor in Amherst Texas---a little Mayo Clinic on the plains. Co-oping may start best with farmers, but a more complex co-op may accompany deeper cultural shifts. Co-op grocery stores may be supported by churches. Churches can learn to do more than weekly sermons. Even better, the media (press and television) monopolies may be partly broken if churches and ethicalists commit to co-ops.

Co-ops sound like an old Christian ideal or perhaps is just a chance idea as we walked out of the Rift Valley on our way to Europe long before Capitalism was an ism. Culture is still up to us---competition easily becomes a cultural disease and not merely a way to produce things. Cultures do change. Before the Amherst co-op, we plowed up the buffalo grass around Amherst just to raise cotton. The plowed soils created the dust bowl that gave me asthma and drove me to Arizona. In the 1990s I visited the Yorkshires in England where our family of Quakers, Methodists and Unitarians have been deep into the cotton mills of the Industrial Revolution. My family in the Yorkshires were deep into the co-op idea and in 1847 helped achieve the Ten Hours Act in Parliament to limit work hours in the mills and start schools within the mills of West Yorkshire.

In Arizona I hope that the Mayo Clinic will widen itself, duplicate the Amherst medical experience, and employ more doctors on a salary basis. A larger project to create co-op owned newspapers and television stations to replace oligarch owners is thinkable. The churches need projects as John Cobb would admit. Methodists and Quakers need a method. Co-oping is the next big American Revolution.

John Fielden

My father, John R. Fielden Sr., and a little gang of farmers used the monkey wrench to create the Amherst Co-op Hospital in a very small town in West Texas. The town was already co-opist with a co-op cotton gin and gas station. The American Medical Association did forbid doctors being employees, but the success of the Co-op did suggest ways the great plains could reverse the wrath of the dust bowl and have grapes instead. Over the years, ways to preserve the aquifer has included growing grapes instead of irrigated crops that use more water. The water crisis and the medical crisis were both real. Inspired work with a simple monkey wrench of the mind and the wind now produces electricity and the dust has been turned into silicon chips.

BITE SIZED RELIGION FOR DIGESTION

1. Abraham's anxieties, we now call the post-modern-condition.
2. As Brahma faded, Vishnu is here and Shiva starts female clinics––patience required.
3. Yahweh tried and tried to build a nation and Jeremiah stayed home in Egypt for new starts. Desert tribes, without rivers, are in steady crisis at every border.
4. Rome was a Caliphate before it was a failed symbol, but lives on in Woody Allen's movies.
5. The Greeks moved slowly westward past Vesuvius to Florence for art and justice.
6. Rome burned but did need Nero's canal to the Bay of Naples that was denied.
7. Machiavelli was for the new Athens, but had bad years when the Rhine froze over.
8. The 'West' was always west of Athens and Jerusalem and over the Alps.
9. Rome's historians have always had to admire their bread and circus, as up-to-date-psychology for happy robots.
10. The English navy defined Protestantism for the Tudors, but at last became the tool of sinful colonialism.
11. The Ten Hours Act of 1847 by Parliament, defined later Protestantism for the Jesus Movement.
12. America was impure but the Puritans signed on to a flawed Constitution to be amended.
13. The holy-wind that blew the Spanish fleet away did not end colonization---today Spain and England are both 51st states of the United States.

14. Foreign Policy is barely foreign---it starts with colonial lust and almost ends with NATO being poorly funded.

15. Churches need Round Tables and not just pulpits---Ghost Ranch is a reconciling Church.

16. Scholastics never give up hermeneutics in their effort to counter road-side evangels and high-church-pretenders.

17. Stanley Hauerwas is a Protestant at Duke U., but with his wife on Sundays he is a low church Methodist and a let-us-pray-Mennonite.

18. In Las Cruces, the Round Table Unity group, shares money and space with the pulpit and allows philosophy to creep in to save the church from itself.

19. Jefferson's dual polity or church and state was the same as Paul's, but Jefferson spent too much time in architecture.

20. What U.S. Protestants protest now, is not the English navy, but the slave ships that ran along side to ruin the dream.

21. Would Yahweh sign on to the U.S. Constitution written on Mount Philadelphia?

22. Why is amending the commandments so hard---they were written to psych-up help in invading Canaan, as they were ordered earlier to invade Egypt and to hold on as captives in Babylon.

23. Is a Jesus Seminar inevitable---Paul's church did protest secular singularity and the church has internal dynamics every Sunday---welcome to ironic complexity.

24. Abraham lived in ironic complexity along with Kierkegaard---so why not build co-ops and change the program?

25. The second coming, for Albert Schweitzer, was delayed so he could expose the clever slavers who would save souls and golds in the Congo.

26. In the life-world, Schweitzer is kin to German idealism, which says human consciousness is as real as silicon and better supportive of a synthetic intellect. In the long run a more complex language is what Harvard would share as part of the synthesis power of intellect.

27. If Kierkegaard were alive today he would marry the girl, feel less anxious and join the Danish co-ops to help save Europe

from corporate-ego-culture. Can co-ops both support and save capitalism from itself?

28. If Protestants can't protest theocracy alone, why not join the Ford Foundation and Catholic Maynard Hutchins at the Center for the Study of Democratic Institutions?

29. To learn to read, could we rethink the Grapes of Wrath from the view of the wrath and no grapes---is context missing in the public schools?

30. Spinosa, saw himself replacing Calvin and Newton with love of God or nature, and this allows hand holding Christians to sing in a circle with the new social scientists who claim new correlative statistical truths and a larger budget for science at the University or Multiversity.

31. Can Barnes and Noble and George Orwell save us from eclectic readers. Could we be saved from reading the late news from the end of the barn, directed by pigs pivoting on hind legs as the local press?

32. Can Ed Abbey's Monkey Wrench book help us reflect past football and the computer?

33. Would Sunday School be saved by a pubic reading of the New York Times on Sunday just outside the pulpit?

HELLO FAREED ZAKARIA---YOU CAME
LATE TO AMERICA--1970-S

1. American students had rebelled against draft laws---why was America acting like a world empire? He found the students were now beaten into technology-math and science labs for jobs. Enchantment with life has been replaced by ideology of free-enterprise and stoic adjustment psychology, along with sports, bread and circus culture.

2. Cheap Hollywood movies suggest new science worlds, perhaps in outer space or other space. Zakaria spends no time with science theories----does not mention Whitehead, Heidegger, Sartre, Rorty and Niebuhr. Spinosan romantics are left out along with big-history, philosophy and world religions. Uncritical history is left to coaches and Lynn Chaney.

3. The liberal churches are tax free and could fight back but they appear empty and the largest choir wins. At least in foreign policy, my friends are teaching foreign policy at a large Methodist Church in Phoenix. If foreign policy and the State Department are left to Ivy Leaguers and legacy students and frat students like the Bushies, we will need Emerson's over-soul to save us from Harvard. Emerson did suggest that blowing clover would be a better sermon topic than most Harvard sermons and Bible dramas. The churches can do sun and wind community grids and give space for defense lawyers---they could start DVD University free courses.

4. Politics in America consists of more than 'centering' with David Brooks---the Clintons came between the Bushies---they were FDR Southers, but today the South is hopeless and there is nothing to triangulate but the big banks who prefer low taxes, power

and money as national policy. The Clintons hope Oboma can secure the Latin vote for them. The Clintons can help the gender revolutions and make day-after pills available in rural pharmacies. There are ways to unscrew the South and the Clinton's are screw experts.

5. The world includes Zakaria's India where the techno-math revolt is underway. Pluralist India has always been in trouble with neighbors who don't believe in nation building. The Indian Hindu Party, like the old Commies in Russia and China are angry nationalists. Russia has been threatened forever at every border by Mongols and theocrats.

6. Welcome to the U.S. Empire that is fading like the Roman Catholic Church. Can the Protestants and Catholics help re-enchant the Western World and can NATO function to make the world and American peace mostly one?

7. Zakaria may be too recent to America to deliver us from various evils---NATO needs our money, India needs patience with democracy, China needs time to recover from colonialist evils, Russia needs time to burst past the old blockades to the warm oceans. Welcome to America––it is not hopeless, but is complex. One help may get us past what Eisenhower called the Military-Industrial-Complex-Psychology. As complex language studies available in dictionary devotions at home and in the Socrates Café down the street and in Church Sunday Classes converted to classes everyday free and open.

John R Fielden

WHY TRAVELERS SELDOM KNOW
WHERE THEY ARE OR HAVE BEEN ITALY
AS AN IMPORTANT EXAMPLE

Most people have heard of the Mafia, the Pope and some famous churches---this is crap. Some know the names of artists and their works and styles---more crap. This is little more meaningful than a trip to the California beaches and the land of shallows.

Italy is a flow of Greek culture westward and of complex Christian unity issues versus the Germanic tribes. Unless you know what Greek culture and Greek problems were, the flow west is trivial. Italy is part of the Greek flow into France and Europe---without history, Italy is a tourist trap. My friend had a years leave and scholarship to Florence but studied mostly the whores and the artists. At the University of California he awed the professors with his notes on Florentine art. He remembered there were Etruscans north of Rome––they were of a mysterious origin and served as a grainery for Rome. A few trees and no flow---most travelers do not know where they were or are. Minus a rich history and cultural contexts Italy is like a trip to the California beach towns or a movie of thin plots made just behind the beaches.

Meaning involves contexting and backing up beyond the present as presented in lab datas, social surveys or travelers 'out the window notes describing countryside'. Descriptions without theory and historical contexts are thin things that poorly educated reporters do for their editors. Americans should not be allowed to travel abroad directly from their Arizona ranch. No-context Americans went to no-context schools. The wide intellectual world is wide because a great deal happened before George Washington and the computer. Try connecting the Po river flood zone to the precarious safety of Italy----try protecting Florence in the Arno valley compared to the context of hill towns like Sienna. Try to understand that Pisa, down the Arno, made Galileo famous for no-context travelers who have no inkling of the meaning of the Greek Renaissance up river.

Let the churchers pray for meaning as well as good cameras and a tourist bus. What does Italy mean? Sensate datas are called 'presentational immediacies' by Whitehead---by this he meant to give up on much of his earlier biased education which was mostly numbers and descriptions. Numbers and descriptions have a place---sometimes heavily biased towards the visible. Ignorance can be spelled differently---numbers and descriptions are important biases and when they fill education they tell you that you are not ready to travel with the meanings folks.

Tuscany has the walled city of Lucca near Pisa. They have recently banned fast food (ethic foods) in their historic center inside the walls. Lucca has a long tradition of self-preservation. When Italy was unified in the 1860s, Luccans pooled resources and bought the walled city from the new nation, to prevent it being torn down. Rome wants the tourist to come and will risk fast foods. Lucca resists because they are Etruscans and not Romans. Lucca traces back to the Etruscans 108 B.C before Rome took over. There is more than a leaning tower in Lucca.

In the Italian Renaissance, Greek time is human acting---creating-synthesizing possibilities beyond math time and physics time or lines, points and edges. In Renaissance time Plato was a model builder of the possibles (and not a dreamer of perfect forms only) and Aristotle was a biologist-politician concerned with the polis beyond individual perspectives---his four causes focused on the core needs of a city and still considered individual potentialities as a dynamic left open to actual living experiences. In Italy, Savanarola and Machiavelli sought ways to defend the hill-towns as small republics (little Athens)---the artists challenged three dimensionality by moving the frames like flow charts----they rediscovered time as a part of human being. Euclid's three dimensional universe was useful but inadequate for a world of human biological and political dynamics. Some artists sold biblical scenes to the Vatican and slipped in some Greek humanist interests at the margins. They were turning Italy into a Greek experiment far beyond the original rocky Greek homeland. To say they discovered a fourth dimension (time) is to say that exploring human nature and human potentials slowly came in various epochs or historical bubbles---the Greeks helped reveal some aspects of human nature to themselves and the gods. History may be causal in places and situations as a revelation of human problems and the nature of human being.

John Fielden

THE THREE KEY GREEK PHILOSOPHERS
IN SOME WAYS THEY ARE ONE
SOCRATES---PLATO---ARISTOTLE

1. For Parmenides, there is no real change---only apparent change and or cultural change in the cave of our habits and rituals. For Heraclitus all is change or flux---so you can't step into the same stream twice. For Thales and pre-Socrates, atoms are the only reality---this extreme positivism was held for moderns by Francis Bacon.

2. Intuited democracy can be demonstrated in babies denied in an ice cream test---so all of us are born democrats, but loss of democracy over time and situations can also be demonstrated empirically or in historical and geo-political realities.

3. For Marcel Proust, facts do not find their way into the world where our beliefs reside; they did not produce our beliefs; they do not destroy them; they may inflict on them the most constant refutations without weakening them.

4. Plato was for women's equality, so that ways of limiting women are expected in the culture wars or the culture caves we live in. For Plato, the state is responsible for the ego or self of children who are without family ego formation advantages. Plato's eternal forms may be democracy, even if democracy is difficult to hold once started. On going attacks on democracy involve attacks on Socrates' justice system---this means we need ways to alter unjust first position contracts, as modernist John Rawls agrees.

5. Democracy in Athens was unlikely as a small and agriculturally poor areas with many tribals near by. Plato noted that culture cave habits threaten the democracy of free persons. Ways to focus

cultural criticism on the cave, he would call philosophy, or in our schools the Humanities. Critical studies of the state of democracy is limited geo-politically and by dirty tricks of big interests among which are tribalists or the military industrial complex that is willing to use 'fear itself' to increase power and pull taxes from the commons. Education wars are part of our critical reality in the view of Plato and Reinhold Niebuhr. Education, as a class and nationalist propaganda, tries to return the nation to tribe or nationism. Niebuhr might liturgize ways to defend a critical realist basis for public education. Urbanizing America needed critical realism in our schools thought Niebuhr and C.W. Mills. Mills saw the cave of happy-robots being sold Rome-like as patriotism in the public schools. Psychology adjusted cavers, in the urbans, have no assurance of jobs, so they vote as 'independents', which means they hide their views to keep their jobs and vote on personalities or not vote at all.

6. One way to undermine education is to say there is no real history and so knowledge is only metaphor or language only that Sophist (lawyers) call real power. The power of original constitutions and courts to deny democracy caused the Whig Republican, Abraham Lincoln, to feel the need for a philosopher preacher like Theodore Parker to help us understand what Emerson, in his Divinity School sermon, meant by miracles that are more like wind in the clover. Unfair contracts, like the contract in Philadelphia, can be changed over time and in defined political space, as Aristotle would call the nation.

7. Nation building, for the Greeks, was interrupted by Alexander and the Romans, and not helped by liturgizing holy places as did the Hebrews---the Italian-Greek Renaissance helped, but the geo-politics of Italy did not give democracy a full chance. The Greeks were back in the center as French, German and English thinkers took on the dictators and theocrats---and we are still at it.

John R Fielden

RENE DESCARTES---CAN HE BE SAVED FROM HIS DREAM OF PERFECT KNOWLEDGE---1590-1650----THE VATICAN WAS ALWAYS WATCHING

1. The church is a form of complex co-operation or thinking therefore it is or has a form of I am real. The 'I am' of Aristotle involves potentials and human made value propositions-- therefore we are a thinking thing or cognizant---for Plato this meant we create values over atomic facts, for Aristotle it meant looking for new potentials for complex cooperation and for Socrates it meant contracting with the state to correct unfair first position contracts.

2. Thinking the I Ams involves ideal relations, and as Anselm noted, this is not merely a concept about having concepts. Can the churches enlarge complex co-operation by using economic co-ops to alter the effects of economic competition in the creation and distribution of goods----goods that include varied media ownership or points of view media? This was George Orwell's concern in Animal Farm and 1984. For Anselm we can reset socio-economics relations---we can define problems and possible solutions as public policies.

3. Descartes, with Galileo, has two books (one to please the Pope) For Descartes there are two natural realities---bodies and minds and the problem of overlap or synthesis of the two---Aristotle called it psycho-somatic relations. After Aristotle a long Hellenistic era sought the Plotinus 'one'----where all of nature was an elaboration out of God, and played with stoic psychology or adjustment to replace the Greek philosophers---this was roughly from 300 B.C. to 1300 A.D. The Hellenistic stoics were cognizant about nothing and oneness being the same---we may call it tautology or circular

thinking and some would call it analytic or 'merely' a definition of terms. Both synthesis along with analysis of terms without propositions, may be just noise.

4. Kant's mental concepts involve noumenal help to bracket out and bracket in phenomena of the extended world. For Kant we are born cognizant of good will and free will---we may call these concepts that Descartes would leave merely to the I Am of our minds---philosophers call this the theory of ontology or being that can not be detected in science labs about our being. Kant's analysis starts with concepts that are dual with noumenal energies serving as synthesizing---he got rid of body and mind synthesis and turned it all to a concept war between human will and good will. His ethics or good-will may be seen as noise.

5. Medievalist Peter Abelard defined reality as love and grace---this is tautological logic or logo-centric and tells us more about the author---with Spinosa he claims a oneness of God or nature that when repeated produces the Subaru-love effect. Subarus are for gentle black forest roads and not the big fare from Munich to Berlin. For Abelard and Spinosa, God or nature solves the synthesis issues of mind and body differences. This view may leave the object world as empty as Plotinus and as Aristotles' search for potentials where nothing is proposed until a potential is propositional in public policies.

6. In modern philosophy, Heidigger and Sartre-Husserl, would project ideals into the actual world. Whitehead likes this even if the actual is complex with corporations having more actual effects than the churches and the Kantian idealists who are quasi Plotinus. Quasi Plotinus includes Christian liberals like Scliermacher whose pietists would reduce god and the one to God-Consciousness. Lutheran nationalism as a quasi theocracy did not like this anti-sectarian mindism. German nationalism and Catholic theocracy have much in common---Hitler found this sectism an open road to power. Whitehead's actual world may be concretion language and no concrete----if you say process over and over, will it include god––love and grace in the Subaru of life?

7. For Descartes, what exists is not God but an Anselm-like-definition of God as perfection or a collection of all goods---this perfect definition of a perfect being is circular and a tautology of self referencing or truth by definition---a synthesis of actual things, so treated, we may call the analytic of terms. Anselm's attributes or predicates are aggregates of actual things that Plato would call values. Descartes' god is dead, not on arrival but by definitional status only. If God is not part of the synthesis and only a product of synthesis as a dream spirit, he has no way to live in Whiteheads-god-to-be.

8. If God is like a triangle he still needs consequences outside the triangle---he needs a cleaning service. God, like sex, involves complexity---merely penetrating god by prayer may be too strong when we only need to petition. A subjective knowledge of god is not a knowledge of God but of subjectivity---Anselm would add all the good thoughts-qualities and claim god is present in the added, but how his claim that knowing god and sex is like a triangle is available for non triangles is unclear. Sexuality varies from flirtation to penetrations and gets us into Locke's claim that power and reality is reasonable but not simply reason. We know that social security has reasonable consequences that are roughly measurable and alterable via elections. Jesus was social but not specific on social laws---flirtation is not simply sex, and God is not known by definition of his trianularity. Descartes was too focused on being clear and distinct---he and god need to focus results or consequences, and not live by words and love babble alone.

TO BE AND TO KNOW---- CLEAR KNOWING CHALLENGED BY PASCAL-BAYLE HUME ROUSSEAU HEIDEGGER-HUSSERL SARTRE OPPENHEIMER---LOCKES REASONS WITH A SMALL R---A SET OF NEW DEALS NEGOTIATED

1. Descartes' France was not a democracy but a king-priest theocratic class and a violent revolt in 1789. Real protest in Locke's industrial new deals---was in the 1847 Ten Hours Act. The Lockean system mixed the social gospel (new deals) with courts to protect the poor---labor unions and other negotiations were added in time.

2. Pascal, an earlier inventor of the computer, turned away from science and scientism without moving to Paul's dual polity public policy system----Pascal was too early to try the Lockean system and so turned to a leap of faith to the here-after and missed the leap of faith to democracy that was happening in England. Pascal was right to be wary of scientism that Spinosans were spreading across Europe as a romance of God-or nature, which is a perfect confusion and anti-intellectual use of language midst the wish for perfect knowledge from God.

3. Pierre Bayle, for the French Hugenots, hid in Rotterdam to write and reveal his doubts about salvation by church doctrines and ceremonies---he said clear knowledge was not the way of Yahweh who negotiated for a strong and morally flawed King David in the great task of building a nation midst tribals so Yahweh gets credit for an early try at nation building midst a mad culture of tribals between the rivers (Nile and Euphrates). In the west, German tribes were famous for over-defending their borders---Bismarck

used political and social gospel tricks to almost unify Germany and Hegel used the claim for a new world-spirit moving past the tribals for new mental unity. The Germans almost made unity under Wiemar but the heavy way that Wilson and the west ended World War One made it most likely that Nazi and Communist tribes would take Germany into World War Two.

4. The 17th century Enlightenment started with Descartes claim for clear and distinct knowledge to replace the bewildering claims of witches and mystics for truth, but Descartes fell into a new dualism (like the two books of Galileo) and a search for a clear synthesis was left up to heaven---bodies and minds were not clearly one.

5. Spinosa put the finish to clear and distinct claims to know---his romantic God-or nature was a kind of synthesis that humanist Jews like Spinosa, Unitarians, Kantians and in time corporations could use and was what Emerson called the Over-soul ---a way we could know deity like corporations know God as the free enterprise over-soul truth.

6. Various moderns like Martin Marty have tried a synthesis of mind and body with a focus on the social gospel---pietist Schliermacher did it early in Germany as a kind of liberal Protestantism not unlike Wesley's and Borg's love song today.

7. Process thinking in Cobb-Whitehead, Jung and Chardin have turned world loyalty into a kind of Kantian salvation formula--- where good will and noumena interrupt phenomena in their quasi science---god or nature psychology of adjustment to the great what is. Holy Joe Campbell and Bill Moyers are finding signs everywhere as part of god-or nature messages.

8. Hume and Rousseau added their complexity to knowing as did Schopenhauer with his quasi romanticism of will and feeling that finds a way via music to defy the physics world determinists. Heidegger Husserl and Sartre added existential selves and social towardsness as ways to complex modern thinking---Quakers and Methodists vaguely joined the English Unitarians to negotiate with Parliament a social contract for the poor in the 1847 Ten Hours Act---union and elections were urged but England fell into colonialism and land grants from the king that delayed their

negotiations with the social gospel. The nasty coal industries, and loss of two world wars, turned England into a mere 51st security colony of the rising United States. The U.S. claimed to have won the two world wars.

9. Today, Richard Rorty and Habermas are for negotiations without Kant's noumenal good will energy claims and Borg and Wesley mystical Spinosan' scientisms---new deal Greek dialectic projects are the best offer of Rorty pragmatists and Habermas' language action society. Process thinkers are accused of psych adjustment and a new capitalist world order----where competitive attitudes, taught early, work like Spinosan god or nature to create a free enterprise reality---thus turning scientism into a mind-set for makers and producers as Adam Smith's god or nature claim.

10. Emerson's over-soul claim for American manifest destiny was easy to sell---Presbyterians moved their version of nation building to the American southwest frontier---the industrial revolution in Scotland did not work as Robert Owens and others hoped. Owens new world order in New Harmony Indiana did not work. Big factory feudalism in the English midlands did not work well, even with Parliament getting on the side of the poor in the 1847 Ten Hours Act.

11. German unity was given up by Bonhoeffer's vague 'process' sermons on world loyalty––the vagueness of process---the 'en' in pantheism is a way to bring Spinosa and Kant to war against Darwinist and Galileo single book truth claims---while at the same time using science optimisms and the gadget wars to distract public attention to more gadgets.

12. Reinhold Niebuhr warned Bonhoeffer that the German problem was deeper than a process sermon and warned the U.S. that nationalism here was not a solution to our crisis when mixed with claims of puritans for our manifest destiny. The German problem was tribal but still half hidden in the Lutheran and Roman sects that were claiming their theocratic sects were chosen from on high.

13. Sartre and the Existentials want us to cease living in abstractions and try more testable projects within the safety of democratic elections. Can we have democratic elections if the tribals and

fear-itself dominate the world---and especially the United States where slavery attitudes hang on and Cold War psychology has corporate connections----more and better weapons are for sale---we sell only the second best to allies who then depend on us for replacement parts.

14. Arthur Schopenhaur added doubts about any universal determinist will and claimed human desires and feelings are more basic than Kant's good will and can help us define what we know---he claimed we can know the self in terms of effects of will and not just by good will or any claim of science for a determined physically willed universe.

John R Fielden

WHAT IS MYSTICAL---A FOCUS ON CHRISTIANITY AND CRISIS OR THE NEW REALITY OF THE LATE MIDDLE AGES MEISTER JOHANNES ECKHART (1260-1327) AND THOMAS AQUINAS (1225-1274)

In the late 13th and early 14th centuries Meister (Master) Eckhart and Thomas Aquinas were Dominican brothers. Dominicans were to specialize in speaking to town folks in the crisis era of European change or the breakdown of the feudal system. In the new towns a new class (bourgeois) business society was breaking away from the agricultural middle ages. The church was in danger of losing contact with the new town peoples. Not only was the Italian Renaissance (new and old Greek ideas) moving north in Europe but places like Cologne and Paris were centers of the new change. In Paris the academics, including Thomas Aquinas, were still at work on logic and cosmologies centered in the omni powers of the deity. Augustines's City Of God and City of Man seemed on the edge of a new challenge.

In Cologne, Meister Eckhart saw a rising 'merchant mentality' as an ultimate sin. Eckhart's views suffered from an inquisition in Cologne (1320s)---when the Archbishop of Cologne accused Eckhart of favoring the German provinces over the German Emperor. Beyond the church walls Eckhart joined the Beghard Society that focused on rising class tensions. Eckhart claimed the landed nobles and new bourgeois failed to recognize the nobility of peasants---some of whom were moving into the towns as craftsmen. Class is a mystical concept that requires an intellectual leap past logic, cosmologies and physical atoms. Thomas Aquinas moved about from Paris to Cologne and Italy (born in Naples) and was under fire from neo-Platonists who wanted to ignore the City of Man that Augustine had given temporary status. Neo-Platonism had for ages focused on Plato's forms that could be seen as God's truths which we could not attain in practical human situations. The actual Plato and Aristotle were focused on the polis and new problems which Aquinas identified as the crisis of 'just prices'---monopoly prices could undermine food prices in the new towns. Aquinas was announcing a new arena of economic ethics for the church to deal with. Augustine had recognized the 'city of man' had legitimate problems to deal with, but they were supposed to pass away as the church grew in power. Just prices sounds difficult to settle in simple physical or atomic terms. Eckhart would move the debates about reality from logic and cosmology and atoms to social and political novelty. Science could not settle or even understand matters of class and fair or moral economics in the commons or polis of life. Aristotle re-discovered in the Italian Renaissance cities (Greeks moving west and north) can be seen as a metaphysics or deeper physics and plan for the polis. Aristotle's empirical view was that human potentials are dynamic----a complex set of ideas, interests and abilities that can't be settled by faith-statements of Augustine and the cosmologies and logics of scholastics in Paris. In modern terms Eckhart would say that science and business interests do not have the right methodologies to discover the actual world of human dialectics and conflict of interests---business and science are sources of ignorance and only pretend to be knowledge industries. The old certainties of Augustine that the City of God would win over the City of Man was just simple bi-modal thinking that could pass.

The mystical way to know need not be a denial of the material world but a more complex grasp of it---a deeper view than the shapes outlined on Plato's cave wall. Mystics may deliver a more complex report world that includes our evolving consciousness. Aquinas plus Aristotle and a new Plato gave Christianity a new chance to deal with reality. Cosmological speculations in Paris could be mixed with economic and political reality. Aquinas' connections to Italy were varied---he was born in the old Greek Italy in Naples and made many trips to Italian towns other than Florence. Eckhart thought actual reality involves concretions that are as practical as Plato's concern for ways to contour power-elites in the polis. Land holding nobles and their military allies were especially nervous that the new-rich bourgeois would buy up their lands and demote their status in

France and German agricultural areas. There is no way to grasp such social and political complexity in a science lab---minds develop around history, imagination and serious concerns for the contours of the polis. Science data-machines and mechanical reductions of reality to identified causes is a way to ignorance. Even Newton was unnerved by claims to know that a cause exhausts the effects by mechanical extension of the cause to all knowable effects. Democracy in a polis involves a complex mix of values put forth and tested in the polis. Only a public that follows proposals and tests complex proposals is able to grasp what citizenship in the 'city of man' requires. Democracy may seem mystical to atomists that have injured their minds by counting as real, only what they can count in the short run of the laboratory or cave.

John Fielden

OVERVIEW OF THE LONG HISTORY OF PROTESTANTISM----GREEKS, HEBREWS AND ZOROASTRIANS INCLUDED---ON GOING PROTESTS

1. Three Greeks---Socrates, Plato and Aristotle moved west as did the Hebrews and sects of Zoroaster----Florence and Venice opened the way west.

2. Rome's empire failed but at last joined the Spanish navy and a colonial empire.

3. Protestants failed to protest well in Germany, France and Holland but got their best chance in England's Industrial Revolution---sadly England's great start in the Industrial era (1847 Ten Hours Act) by Parliament and the churches slipped away in the temptation to an English colonial naval empire and the loss of two world wars. The two world wars were the beginning of an American empire and the Cold War. Reinhold Niebuhr and C.W. Mill's critique of the U.S. Empire involves a rethinking of American claims to a Manifest Destiny and a Puritan Utopia. Slavery and state sovereignties are hard to fit into a great commons nation.

4. Philosophy as the interrupted flight of the Owl Minerva has many side interrupts before landing even for the night. New Mexico is a special interrupt in the American scene and involves many New Mexican dirts including the atomic dirt in Los Alamos and the high cultural education of Robert Oppenheimer before he witnessed the bomb in Almagordo and remembered the Indian Gita as the edge of a new reality where Shiva, Vishn and Krsna

open a new protest and negotiation against the old cosmic god Brahma.

5. The American empire shocked Eisenhower as the Military Industrial Complex---too complex for a simple Mennonite from Kansas---and the rise of the American Right from Goldwater to Reagan. Ike proposed positive thinking and others proposed world loyalty and church every Sunday.

6. Germany unity is the big story of Europe––they revived the Greeks but Rome's and Luther's theocratic states made unity difficult and an easy mark for the Nazis. The Nazis had other basis for unity--- Wilson, the big navy and new American empire man had treated Germany badly and simply took over the last of England's empire. England itself became a 51st American state.

7. Various groups proposed new ways for Minerva to negotiate God and history. Process thinkers---Whitehead––Jung and Chardin proposed a new world loyalty, green Jesus or natural religion as Spinosa had done in Europe as a great unifier. Jesus Seminar groups have proposed a metaphorical Jesus or a logo centrism where words are salvic---Marcus Borg has spread this view---saying love and grace over and over replaces all the old ceremonial religions.

8. Others have tried to save God by inventing human concepts like good will (Kantian noumenal language). John Locke, Paul, Niebuhr and Plato have us debating various human interests that may be seen as public policies in the democratic republic for the flight of Minerva. Our interests are univocal and our extreme interests may be seen as sins----Aquinas brought the sense of economic sins to the West as unjust-prices and Socrates' sense of alterable contracts. Meister Eckart proposed craft unions for the new German towns and challenged Rome as the source of social-economic truths.

9. Heidegger, Husserl, Sartre and Kierkegaard proposed democratic leaps midst uncertain anxieties---in the U.S. various new deals have been tested midst the uncertain flight---uncertainty can be tolerated in a democratic republic. Sartre would cure the windbags by testing our projects more concretely. Walter Bruggemann deals with the interrupts of Minerva in negotiation by Yehweh and

David ---negotiating the commons proved most difficult midst the traibals and we need not give up. Germany and Europe are now trying to build a nation with a sovereign banking system and a NATO Military, Russia and the oil sheiks are trying to keep Europe divided and dependent on the U.S. for security.

10. Kant's good-will and Borg's love-produces-love like a Subaru for Minerva. In complex causation the Protestant Churches may focus on opportunities and not just on property contracts. Churches with tax free locations can enter various long term co-opist adventures that will alter the capitalist enterprise flights of Minerva. The courts, media ownership, public education, and police over-sight can be altered by the protesting churches. God bless America can be sung in flight.

WORLD LOYALTY IS AN EASY ENCHANTMENT IN NEW MEXICO BUT REINHOLD NIEBUHR AND C. W. MILLS SAW SERIOUS DISTRACTIONS IN THE CRISIS OF COLD WAR NATIONALISM MIDST THE DIFFERENT DIRTS OF NEW NEW MEXICO

1. I tried to enchant the plains in an earlier book while I did seminars at Ghost Ranch in the summers ---I knew the Craft Villages were having hard times and that holy dirt did not solve all the problems for the nobodies there midst the somebodies at Ghost Ranch. In Ghost Ranch I met preachers like Larry Rasmussen who was retired from Union Theological School in New York---he spoke in church terms for liturgies of enchantment.

2. Different dirts have a kind of sermon of their own. East of Cimarron my father and brother delivered cotton seed cake to the ranches over snow drifts and hard times. There was 'holy dirt' in Chimayo and the Blood of Christ mountains---the Catholic Church got there early---there was atomic dirt in the Jemez and Los Alamos---here Oppenheimer's early ethical culture education in N.Y. got him accused of leftism by the growing Bircher cults---creeping Fascism even in the land of enchantment. Would Oppenheimer share our secrets with the Spanish besieged in Barcelona by the Fascists? There was Texas oil dirt trying to run the New Mexico Legislature. There was Georgia O'Keefe's red and yellow dirt up the Chama River at Ghost Ranch. There is white-sands dirt with drones and missiles for enemies unknown. There is golf at ten thousand feet in Cloudcroft with a stunning view over the white-sands. There is guano-dirt in Carlsbad in a

world class cave built one drop at a time. There is hippie dirt in Taos arroyas that can make you a world citizen one mud block at a time. The Presbyterians hold forth at Ghost Ranch despite Georgia O'Keefe's objection to a church running the enchantment. In the middle Chama River at Tierra Amarilla---there is the land of the angry Yellow Earthers.

3. There is even strangeness in the enchantment---O'Keefe's cow skulls and single flowers seemed to be an otherness as does the Pueblo nations run mostly by women---otherness and paradox. Earlier Comanchero traders used the cow skull to guide across the llano to sell horses to the Comanches who were besieged in the red canyons south of Amarillo. The Yellow-red dirts of the Palo Dura on the Red River enticed O'Keefe to deeper reds in New Mexico.

4. Otherness is New Mexican---Ted Turner is creating an anti-ranch in the edge of the Black Range and Jane Fonda took on the military industrial complex before Oppenheimer did---she lives on the upper Pecos. New Mexico has a river and a half---if we count the Gila she has two rivers.

5. Roswell has an anti-world theo-other view and escapes to some other dirt---now the Pecos barely runs there. Texan long drives to the market via Roswell ended with the short grass just west of the Inn of the Mountain Gods' apache ski and casino. In Chimayo things to do include carving holy figures, raising donkeys from Spain, crafts, apple trees and ways to avoid selling land to Yankee and Hollywood investors. Ski soils include the light snows of Eagles Nest, Red River, Ski Taos, Ski Santa Fe and the Ruidoso slopes.

6. The Mogollon and Black ranges are canyons to nowhere but to cat-walk and Dude ranching above the Gila---there is not enough water for dudes and Gila monsters seek water from the one cloud rains down in the lower Gila of Arizona.

7. C.W. Mills and Niebuhr would see N.M. in the complexity of the Cold-War and not just in world-loyalty enchantments. Preachers are tempted to choirs, good will and art up to your chantment---and different dirts litugized. The different high deserts of New

Mexico enchant differently and are partly under siege by the U.S. Military and Oil corporations.

8. Sun and wind and nation building are still possible---as in the low thunder in Chimayo of late summer under the apple trees, but there is atom city in the distant Jemez Range and there is Intel of Albuquerque sucking water out of the blood of Christ mountains. A map of New Mexico is a head trip---large cow skulls once guided us across the plains---we now know that enchantment by preachers and corporations are not far from the seep of nationalism. Nation building and nationalism are difficult to keep separated so long as the schools don't work well and the media is owned by corporations. Capitalism is good so long as it doesn't create mostly psychic ills---to counter the extremes of capitalism we need long term strategies that only churches and an Ivy League education can sustain. Enchantment is not just a trip down Canyon Road in Santa Fe.

John Fielden

HOW TO READ THE GREEK ENLIGHTENMENT LONG BEFORE FRANCIS BACON AND THE 17TH-18TH CENTURY ENLIGHTENMENT AND HOW TO READ ARISTOTLE'S FOUR CAUSES AS OTHER THAN THE GREAT CHAIN OF BEING THAT ENDS IN AN APOCALYPSE FOR CHRISTIANS---TRY SEVERAL ENDS THAT ARE NOT FINAL---SOMETHING LIKE THE OWL MINERVA'S NIGHT FLIGHT OF PHILOSOPHY

1. Thomas Aquinas was wrong to see Aristotle's fourth cause as a single final cause or purpose to please the Christians back in Rome----Socrates had proposed a cause for justice in economic relations that we may call contract theory---original contract positions can be negotiated in flight. Plato's interest group extremes can be negotiated via values that are never completely settled in flight---he would moderate the interests, particularly the military-tribal interests and he favored women's liberation into the political processes. Aristotle sought new potentials for complex co-operation and competition in the defined space and time of a nation. Churches and intellectually focused strategic projects can use co-ops to both alter and save capitalism from its extremes.

2. The Greeks were too early to try the English Lockean Parliament as a special version of democracy that has responsible parties testing their values in a time frame. Locke was a deist and not concerned to please Rome with loose world loyalty or god and Reason claims to know where Minerva (teleology) must land. Francis Bacon would give Minerva math and science instructions on where and

when to land. The Apostle Paul made a move to a dual polity politic (state and church) that can be altered in flight. The English Industrial Revolution tested the new dual way to make laws (see the Ten Hours Act of 1847) there Protestant churches challenged the Queens theocratic order or Poor House Way to make workers fit the new industrial feudal state. The Protestant way negotiated a new public policy with the state.

3. The English Parliament moved to a colonial empire and a place to find cotton for the cotton mills in the later 19th century---this failed to negotiate a series of new deals or flight patterns for Minerva within England and resulted in a new nationalism that lost two world wars and left HEW---housing education and welfare, not well negotiated.

4. The Enlightenments need context---then Aquinas found Aristotle's texts in Florence it was clear enough to Machiavelli that Italy was not going to be an integrated nation and northern Europe was a more likely place for Minerva to land next. The crafts and small town revolution of the 12th and 13th centuries was underway and Meister Eckhart in Colonge had already altered the flight of Minerva when craftsmen formed consumer unions and challenged the great land owners and the Roman Church to a new way to be and know. This got Eckhart in trouble with church and state but his Minerva was part of an early enlightenment. France was not a state nor was Germany, but France was a place for Minerva to land differently ---the Popes were placed in French captivity at Avignon while the French state moved variously for Minerva to land there. Eckhart--1260-1327 AD---Aquinas 1225-1274 AD.----the Avignon captivity started in 1305.

5. In Tucson, Joseph Krutch, spoke of the great-chain-of-being where desert animals exhibit survival moves that are as heroic as Hegel's spirit and Minerva---the spirit for Krutch and Edward Abbey helped build the Desert Museum west of Tucson.

John Fielden

YAHWEH, ZEUS AND PUBLIC SCHOOL EDUCATION IN AMERICA--SHALL WE START WITH ZEUS AND YAHWEH IN NATION BUILDING?

1. On our way to Big Bend National Park our Jewish and Catholic pals argued for vocational education and we responded. Public school are busy with art, music, drama, sports and shop courses. Critical national and theory of knowledge is avoided to please the theocratics who came to America is large chunks---and developed new chunks---the on-going Protestant revolution is left out.

2. Spinosa's God or nature came here as a 'scientism' that allows the study of 'nature' as 'science'. Nature includes Darwin's and Newton's 'laws' but instead of laws Darwinism is a loose study of class and individual interests and Newton is turned to space and time as math-physics that avoids political space and time that we create. What is called 'science' is now a sacred cow or ideology in the culture war over military budgets. Plato saw the tribals as military thinking always at war for more guns in the budget.

3. Tax free churches could counter the public school distractions and baby-sitting games. Nations can be studied minus the nationalism of Lynn Chaney, the PTA and sports coaches.

4. Hannah Arendt says Germany needs critical culture history in building a 'commons'---and not just doing it via Kant, Bismarck and Hegel with a capital R-Reason. Germany is now into dialectics or political debate Greek-style---with coalitional Parliaments between regular general elections. Dialectics are other than logo-centric tautologies that simply restate the premise in the conclusion or synthesis. Logo-centrics avoid the critical middle term of dialectics and become mere labyrinths of unthink.

5. German history is part of the Greek and Jewish flow westward. The flow is clearly in patches, with German tribes being more powerful than Rome's Generals. Julius Caesar invaded France and England up to the Scottish tribals and turned back. German unity was given an intellectual boost by Hegel and Marx---the conscious national spirit, long in the making, became a power by 1900. Early in the 19th century German and French thinkers---Heidegger, Husserl and Sartre moved from spirit of nation and class to complex human spirit including gender, race and sect. Germany was late to have a navy and colonies and fought two world wars versus the colonists. The German Republic is now a democracy with a commons---all pay taxes and votes via a Parliamentary system on who spends it.

6. Hannah Arendt says German culture became a banal ordinariness and nationalism which is now shifting to prehend a larger commons in the German Republic. Will the new European commons include Greece and not leave Greece dependent on Russia's forever insecure empire? Public education in the U.S. fails to do the critical dialectic of the Protestant Revolution and falls into banal ordinariness and anti-intellect midst sports, shop education and various science claims to capital T truths in economics theory.

7. A dip into England's 19th century Industrial Revolution can reveal the meaning of 'protest' beyond mere sect and preacher egos. The Ten Hours Act of 1847 joined various Protestant churches and Parliament to deepen what we mean by Protestantism. In the U.S. a delayed industrial revolt occurred because the wide frontier ---free land and ego---reveals ways to avoid the dialectic that has a middle critical term---and has allowed a logo-centrism or labyrinthian way of life that is banal and ordinary. This ordinariness, midst the great military industrial complex that American became, is more important than shop training.

8. Yahweh and Zeus are cosmic originative sources for western civilization---there were tribal wars that Yahweh encountered---Abraham was into gender complexities, Moses was into nation building complexity, Samuel and David were into power moves

and Jeremiah noted the evils of class. Zeus had a dual power and knowledge concern for Apollo and Dionysus. The problem of reason---for Apollo's reason could be with a small 'r'. or an absolute 'R' for Reason. The small 'r' for reason would entertain debate for the male population. Plato wanted to include women in the body politics. Plato claimed a dual complex of interests---he saw the military or tribals at war with those who were mainly reflective. Pericles thought he could share culture with tribes and create the effect of a nation---he also tried a Peace League which would operate as a large tribe but this didn't work well. Greek tragedies may be seen as emotions towards nation building. The Greeks slowly moved west to Europe as did the Hebrews. The Greeks moved to Florence and the Hebrews moved to Germany. German thinkers like Hegel and Kant favored Apollo's Reason---Heidigger, Husserl, along with Sartre and Locke, would focus on reasonable truths that could be debated by Parliament. Nietzsche favored Dionysus and Heidegger favored a towardsness with some anxieties left in. Kierkegaard sought a complex spirit that had the sense of a dialectic and considered a leap to the commons as possible.

9. Post moderns like Sartre and C.W. Mills focused on intents and projects---for Mills a project could be a particular public midst a larger Republic. A particular project and a public could influence a Republic---for examples Berea, Kentucky, Austin, Texas, Tucson Arizona and Boulder Colorado. Churches may work as publics if they adopt long strategic projects or goals with financial ways to test the goals.

FRENCH ENLIGHTENMENT---DESCARTES CLEAR AND DISTINCT--DESCARTES-PHILOSOPOHES DIDEROT AND VOLTAIRE MISSED THE ENGLISH PROTESTANT INDUSTRIAL REVOLUTION---ROUSSEAU RESPONDED

1. The actual Protestant Revolution involved church and Parliament in the Ten Hours Act to limit what corporations can do in the cotton mills of the Yorkshires and Lancashires. England's Industrial Revolution was a clear case of dual polity politics that Paul claimed midst Rome. State churches in Germany and Holland had no such basis for negotiated politics.

2. Politics in late medieval France involved isolation of France from the Spanish-Habsburg-Papal theocracy---isolated France joined the Ottoman Islamics rather than the Protestants of England, Germany and Holland. Toleration of Islamic theocracy actually left France isolated with her own version of theocracy and increasing power of kings acting as local Popes.

3. Jean Rousseau saw French culture causing the French Revolution via class and presumptive theocratic powers in the show-biz city of Versailles. Enlightenment thinker Diderot (of the famous Enclyclopedia of Philosophy) went to Vincennes prison out of suspicion of theocracy. The Philosophes believed 'science' and math but were not clear about God. Rousseau sought to visit Diderot and perhaps get him released on the grounds that that math and science are not in the category 'atheist' necessarily. On the way to Vincennes Prison Rousseau saw a sign advertising a reward for essays that could blur the lines and release Diderot. Rousseau was

a famous musician, dramatist and artist who had operated for his own safety in and out of Geneva Switzerland---he also had a more complex view of the state that we call 'deism'. He won the prize but then his work moved into questions that threatened the King-class system in Versailles. He saw the abuse of art, music and drama in the class courts as theocracy with a nasty claim to class and status. Rousseau became a wanted man and David Hume in England offered the safety of Lockean Parliamentary safety for Rousseau the artist, musician, dramatist in England. The French Revolution was clearly a part of what Rousseau called the general-will of the people. Rousseau challenged the science ideologies as well as the culture distracting politics of Kings and Popes. He said the human 'will' moves things and movement is not the exclusive truth of Newtonian science.

4. The French Revolution was important in breaking the 'science-math-Philosophe-King and Pope rule of France, but it missed the Industrial Revolution in England where the Protestant churches and Parliament made laws minus the smell of theocracy. After Napoleon had passed, August Comte and the French mind-positive math and physics society sought a middle way---they would make the trains run on time and meanwhile partly replace the Catholic Church with a calendar of religious holidays and a chance for civil order based on scientific thinking---if there was a world soul it would have mathematics in it. Comte's positive science spread into Mexico and was called the 'scientificos'. In France Emil Durkheim was the John Dewey of a new solidarity---the skilled workers could unify as least intellectually in something like Spinosa's claim that God or Nature are the same. Dewey was for solidarity but had some actual proposals such as Half-Way homes for the indigent and actual field trips outside of text books to induce student reflections on community differences.

5. American pragmatism for William James was complex----in his book on a variety of religious experiences he noted a difference of 'will' in time and space for the young who had been a spoiled "I" from birth and were moved into a social 'we' briefly in late teen

years. The hard life in a Darwinist economics may have moved the young back to "I-am' quickly. Instrumental pragmatism seemed to have a natural gap in it. Democrat Obama used the personalizing tools of electronic communication to pull the young into 'we-dom' for one election cycle. Wm. James also resisted instrumental pragmatism as American colonialism across the Pacific----where super Christians were used by corporates to create second-class citizens and workers in colonies. Progressive's Teddy Roosevelt and Woodrow Wilson were corporate believers---this could be seen as a deism with religion in clear use as an instrument of power.

6. John Dewey resisted the spectator's reality of the culture mirror as the source of who we are as persons of a society. He was closer to the deist view of Rousseau and David Hume but kept to his more ideological expression of 'scientific Spinosan blur of God or nature, used by R.W. Emerson and the Unitarians. Emerson's 'over-soul' claims an inside tract for truth in the universe. Emerson's logo-centrism simply repeats the conclusion in any premise---love causes love and love is a unity term---if often repeated it becomes part of a labyrinthian certainty---some call this Stoic and or psychological adjustment to what ever is. This solves little because self referencing tautology merely re-states a version of me.

7. Public schools in America generally miss the on-going Protestant dual polity of church and state, where in any historical account of theocracy John Locke's reasonable Christianity and his deism comes down to the best argument wins (dialectics with a critical middle term resists logo-centric truth claims). The best argument in a democratic republic makes laws and alters laws in time and space chosen by our will and not by Newton's god or nature laws.

8. Rousseau reverses the Philosophe enlightenment and places human needs before science-math ideology---he gets the horse before the culture cart clearly but in Paris the King and class culture got their cart before the living horse. Locke's deist god is reasonable and discovers the existential self in stages---we make the general welfare of the commons via institutions like Parliament---we call that public policy.

9. Versailles and Hollywood may distract us with out-west characters for President. John Wayne could have made it---Reagan and Nixon did. Nixon prolonged the Vietnam war and went to China to teach the Chinese his view of peace. It turned out to be more show-biz such as more golf courses to calm the Commies down.

John R Fielden

FOUR OR FIVE GREAT CHRISTIAN RELIGIOUS-POLITICAL-ECONOMIC AWAKENINGS IN AMERICA

1. The first Great Awakening started in the late 17th century when Massachusetts Puritans started to lose control of the frontier settlers---the witch trials may be seen as a desperate effort to discourage Puritans from escaping to the west. By the 1730s and 40s New Light theologies sparred with the Old Light preachers on the coast. In his Northampton church (in western Massachusetts) Jonathan Edwards started to read John Locke on the reasonableness of Christianity. God might be angry at Puritans who were only half-pure or who allowed their mischievous children into church under the sham of a half-way covenant. Edwards in his church started to say that actual behavior and not just faith-statements count. This radical move caused him to lose his ministry in that church and be moved to try out his new light theology with the nearby Indians. This fortunate move allowed him time to read more of John Locke and reasonableness of Christianity. English Puritans decided to be reasonable in the 17 century by starting Parliament as a way to compromise and relative peace.

2. In England, Locke faced the deists who said Christianity contains nothing contrary to reason, but also nothing above reason. Locke was accused of atheism and Socinianism (Unitarianism). Locke was seeking a synthesis of scriptualism and rationalism in reaching towards toleration. In 1696, Edwards attacked Socinianism and Locke replied with a second book on reasonableness. Edwards answered again in 1698. Locke accepted the Bible as inspired by God but he said we have reason for a natural revelation, with self-declared and self-evidenced criteria for the evaluation of truth. This

view is not unlike that of Thomas Aquinas who followed Aristotle in giving nature a chance to be considered before miracles are sought. Edwards kept reading in his semi-retirement and admitted new light on Indian behavior suggested they were scriptureless Christians. As the Puritans lost their frontier there was talk of an American Revolution. A polypiety of Quakers, Calvinists and Puritans of various degrees of purity became the unifying power from Boston south to Virginia---a reasonableness together with some anxiety that England might join the French and give the west to the Indians.

3. Motives for the American Revolution may not have been caused simply by Edwards's new theological light for Indians, the colonies may have gone to war out of fear that the English would allow the Indians to block their way to western lands. In any case polypiety meant the old Calvinist way to salvation by faith statements alone had to give way to faith behaviors. Edwards was invited to be President of Princeton University. It was a bit late---he died within a month but his new awakening was under way. Religious, economic and political revivals tend to mesh---it is not clear that the American Revolution was Lockean but at least Thomas Jefferson quoted Locke as basis for the revolt. If wars tend to come at the end of America's Great Revivals we can begin to see patterns. 17th century English Puritans created and discovered Parliament as a way to peace short of internal war. American Puritans in our first Great Awakening helped create a Parliament-like structure here but one heavily burdened by race and class to be settled later by another war.

4. In we move up one hundred years from the 1740-1760 era of the first awakening to the Second Great Awakening we have another parallel between the English Yorkshires and New England in the beginning of the industrial revolution. Lockean epistemology focused on being born with a blank tablet on which experience could write, but three things were already innately there on the tablet----the rights to life, liberty and property. Liberty and property could not be taken away by the King without due process. The problems of liberty and property have turned out to be difficult to

deal with by calling them 'rights'. Locke's epistemology is called sensationism, empiricism, perceptism, but it is not clear what he or we mean by percepts. Some percepts are isolated or atomic and some are unified by our minds and imagination so are not merely nature's recordings. The mind and our imagination may create and not merely find nature ---in politics and polity we are creators, and the Puritan Parliament may be seen as the greatest creation of Christendom. The church is itself a polity---and in tax-free America, every church becomes a kind of local theocracy. In America each church is more or less democratic and can be more structured around class. The evangelicals, including early Methodists, were more democratic and less structured and today the evangelicals (see Harvey Cox) may be a wave of reviving democracy or a mixed polity from below.

5. Ralph Waldo Emerson in the second Great Awakening (1830-1850) looked past old-light Calvinist preachment to original experience or a hermeneutics beyond the texts in New England and Yorkshire. In 1838 Emerson gave his famous address to the Harvard Divinity School. In 1836 John Fielden in West Yorkshire wrote "The Curse of the Factory System." Fielden was the owner of one of the largest cotton mills at the time and a member of Parliament from Oldham near Manchester. He advocated a limit of ten hours work in all the mills of England and schools to be built within the factories. Ferment was great in the 1830s but Fielden's friend Robert Owens gave up on Parliamentary reforms and started his utopian communes---later in American he built a commune in New Harmony Indiana. The Fielden's agreed with Marx that reform should not be too dreamy and reform should be more than a Methodist song by the Wesleys who were in the neighborhood. The Fieldens (four brothers) who ran the mills around Todmorden on the Calder River were opposed to the "Poor Laws" by which London and Parliament proposed to imprison and correct the bad habits of the poor. Some Poor-laws bureaucrats were dumped into Yorkshire Rivers when they came north to set up their behavioral correction centers. This was a virtual civil war over social policy and how to deal with poverty in the new

industrial system. Methodists proposed singing, Marx proposed revolution, Tories proposed poor laws and Owens proposed setting up model communities or utopias. John Fielden proposed voting rights for all workers and laws to protect the least able from the intimidating poor laws and their moralistic managers. The Fieldens started off as Quakers and moved to become Methodists and then Unitarian Methodists. They built the large cathedral like church in Todmorden and paid the salaries of the first preachers and schools within the churches. Thousands of peasants were being driven from their sheep farms on the moor hills of Yorkshire by something called the Enclosure movement where large estates replaced the small huts of hand-weavers who were forced to work in the more efficient mills. The Fieldens were unable to control the cotton industry by moving their ships to the Carolinas closer to the cotton. New England in the American Revolution was inclined to move the mills to New England and they did. The American Civil War essentially ruined the English mills, but the mills were moving before the war and girls from western Massachusetts were recruited to wage-slavery in New England. In order to join the American union New England had to sign a constitution allowing chattel slavery.

6. The second Great Awakening in America was political, religious and economic––R.W. Emerson and his friends were preachers but most of them gave it up to try another way to earn a living. Only Emerson found a way to live on the lecture circuit and leave the ministry---he and Jon Edwards were lucky to be out of the pulpit and into the great American public. Reform has many sides---Emerson feared English wage-slavery was coming to New England. Calvinist churches (called Old Lights) were not willing to rethink religion. German language and theology (idealism) was in revolt against the mere empiricism of Hume and Locke. Swedenborgians were pitching a new mystic interiority that would avoid what they called "being parasitic on British senasationism-empiricism-or perceptionism." Emerson's first book 'Nature' sought the naked eyeball view of nature (transparency) minus cultural biases that had accumulated over centuries---he would

use original experience unfiltered by culture---this is something like the claims of modern thinker Edmund Husserl who claimed a reflective phenomenology can reveal nature directly in our consciousness before cultural contaminations. Emerson's claim for experience may be seen as Locke's unity of perceptions which we call 'mind', imagination and the making of values. Emerson argued that some unique human problems can not be dealt with by Swedenborg's mystic visions. Emerson claimed chattel and wage slavery are value related problems along with 'will' problems that enter via original experience.

7. Emerson's friends, like Fieldens' friend Robert Owens, were trying to start over with ideal communes like Brookfarm near Boston. Emerson refused to move to a utopian community or to remain a preacher on salary---he and friends started a rent-free location at his home in Concord, Massachusetts which they called the Transcendental Society. Emerson and friends resisted Swedenborgians tying every action to scripture---a new man in a new land might have original experiences---so said Emerson at his Divinity School blast. Emerson saw an original experience of nature before culture and church hermeneutics shaped our views---he sought experience closer to poetry where feeling and spirit was not just something abstract called reason. Reason could be followed to help test out values and spirit, but was not to be confused with spirit. German romantics spoke of spirit often and in a kind of nationalist way. Americans came to speak of spirit here as a 'manifest destiny' Emerson's friends (Thoreau, Ripley and Brownson) would carve out a theology of behaviors---as Locke and Edwards had begun, but they also sought a theology to confront the Old Light Calvinists who still spoke of miracles and frontier optimism without any reflection on an American original philosophy. Emerson was anxious that the wide American frontier could simply dissolve into a philosophy of violence and instrumental utility with materialism in the saddle and riding mankind. There was some help from English thinkers (Samuel Coleridge) who said the innate or fixed mental categories of Kant

were only beginning frames for experience and original reflection in the conscious mind---and so are not finished reflections.

8. Emerson and friends finally turned Unitarianism into several views but the central view was that Jesus was focused on ethical relations regarding others and not with church relations and churches as theocratic power centers. Truth was available in all places and not just in declared holy places by people wearing robes. Some post-Kantian German thinkers came to speak of "will'---William James refocused it on 'free-will'. Hegelians argued that history or human values, when focused, creates more history and doesn't merely find God and the frozen presence in place and time. Some left-wing Hegelians were as open as Emerson's new way in a new land but Hegel lacked the English Parliament to keep the history making dialectic forming policy and statue laws. In the 1830 to 1850 era we may see the ferment in England's Yorkshires and in New England as Great Awakenings. In England it meant eventually that all males could vote and labor unions could organize. In America wage-slave problems were overwhelmed by issues of regional strife over chattel slavery. John Calhoun (Vice President) threatened to keep English cotton mills going using a South Carolina's veto (nullity) of U.S. tariff laws. Andrew Jackson told Calhoun that nullifying U.S. laws would bring federal troops to nullify the nullifiers. The period 1865 to 1900 is often referred to as the 'robber baron' era or the 'gilded age'. The American Civil War ended chattel slavery but one party rule during this long period turned the wide west and the South into commodity colonies serving the factories of New England.

9. If the first two awakenings ended in wars with mixed reform results they at least helped finish off 'faith without works' theology except in the most rural areas. What could a third, fourth and possible fifth awakening be about? In the post civil war era (1865-1900) western farmers populists from Nebraska to Texas started to awaken with some anger and Theodore Roosevelt tried to settle them down by threatening everyone including corporations that he would build an empire for farmers' markets. With a two-ocean navy he would find the way to Asia that Columbus failed to find.

A wave of populist anger reached from Kansas and East Texas to Alabama and Georgia in a way that scared the Democratic racist party more than it unified them---mixing black and white farmers faltered (democratic populism collapsed in the deep south's racism in the 1890s) and finally the Republicans beat Wm. J. Bryan, making Wm. McKinley president and then Theodore Roosevelt replaced the fallen McKinley. But the poor poured into New York from Europe and to Hells Kitchen. American Protestant churches were preaching a version of Social Darwinism and Walter Rauchenbusch preached a counter social-gospel in his Hell's Kitchen church. The exploitive post-Civil War age was associated with the war that had freed the Negro but in 1876 a 'deal' sold him back into a deal for the segregated South and there was no deal for the poor pouring into New York. After Populism, Roosevelt and Woodrow Wilson tried to ignore the farmers and focus on progress in the cities. Wilson's progressivism fell apart in World War One which was fought not simply for peace but for U.S. trade rights in war zones. We claimed to win World War One --- we got there late and we may argue that Wilson's background in American history was not sufficient to understand the tensions left hanging between Islamics and Eastern Orthodox Christians in south eastern Europe---ignorance of religious history is more than simple ignorance.

10. What to do for a fourth Awakening as the last one was lost in the 1920s when the League of Nations was ignored by three Republican Administrations. Reinhold Niebuhr traveled to Europe to view vast cemeteries resulting from World War One. He said, in neo-orthodox terms—a renewed sense of human capacity for evil had been lost in the optimistic determinism of progress and Social Darwinist rhetoric to Niebuhr sin is on all sides and we need to back off of empire building where pride-hubris tempts perceived winners. Winning is dangerous if the culture of winners has little sense of history. Hitler and the Communists opened the new war. Could the New Deal of Franklin Roosevelt win such a war and could we go beyond the progressives and include black persons in the New deal as Mrs Roosevelt proposed? The South was angry at

such views but also proud of their new military bases. They waited out the war before turning against the Roosevelts and the New Deal. Niebuhr's fourth awakening is that the United States and Europe, without wars and hegemonic bragging and with a realistic view of human sinfulness could begin to claim again the sweet old innocence of our higher angels.

11. Do we need a fifth Great Awakening based on peace (Europe seems close to that view) and give up neo-conservative views that God appointed us to spread democratic capitalism to the world---one problem being that we are not sure that capitalism brings democracy into being in any simple way. Democracy came to England primarily because the English Puritans gave up theocracy for Parliamentary processes. Religion and not economics may be seen as the engine of deep changes in the West. The neo-conservatives, and especially their neo-liberal pals, seem to say that free-market economics is the voice of God and nature. Others see an American awakening for peace over guns and our need to use any of our value-surpluses to help other nations towards family planning, free education and new technology that is not forever tied up in patents. The United States might become a hegemon among other hegemons (hegemons are large states with influence-spheres around them which they claim are approved by God). Europe and China may qualify as hegemons along with the United States. We might become a shining city of a hill that Europeans call Sweden.

12. Niebuhr, like R. W. Emerson and Edwards gave up on having their own churches and became thinkers, readers and ethicalists---this tells us something of how religion is not the same as the churches. Great Awakenings challenge old structures and stir new masses to reforms. Puritan polypiety helped reform America 1740-1790 but ended in a war that had something to do with seizing Indian lands to the west and it brought forth some of John Locke's reasonable Christianity in the form of Jonathan Edward's new light theology based on observable behavioral criteria that could seek a community consensus or secular language of compromise. We call this compromise the Constitution. In the 1830 to 1850

era Unitarians pushed behavioral criteria as well as Emerson's Transcendental venture into creative imagination as a factor in behaviors---the material frontier---Indians included, should seek a consensus on the evils of the factory system (wage-slavery) and chattel slavery. The abusive move of railroads and armies across Indian lands 1890-1920 brought a third wave of religious reflection beyond Emerson's creative imagination and to the Social Gospel that recognized the deeper ills of wage-slavery. Class evils had not been solved by the Civil War---a new and wider war developed around colonialist nations seeking commodities for their factories. Race issues were not ended by a Civil War over slavery. Issues of 'class' continued into a fourth Awakening where Niebuhr struggled to separate both race and class from Communist and Fascist mind-sets. Niebuhr thought pragmatic behaviors and inner resolve to compromise and peace required a larger sense of sin than individual sins only---nation groups and their prides (nationism) he saw as a new problem even for Locke's reasonable Christians---reason is not reasonable when theocratic prides invade the consciousness. In any fifth Awakening the United States and Europe may turn any surplus values to peace and need not even democracy and God as a reason to claim we are chosen. Wars may follow and even be caused in some sense by our great religious-moral awakenings, but the greatest awakening may be that human behaviors, however flawed, can be turned slowly from mystical tribal and private claims of redemption to the polis with a commons consensus---a commons that is never complete but has no second class citizens and has the Lockean 'reason' working to judge our inalienable rights as alienable to the extent that property does not have the right to abuse workers, nor the right to own the opinion media. Lockean reasonableness is best focused on life as inalienable and liberty (equated to owning the media as free speech) is somewhat alienable as is property.

13. The fifth Great Awakening is ours to make. History is not merely found, and is partly made. Our great American heroes were not generals or business tycoons. They were Jonathan Edwards, R. W. Emerson, Walter Rauschenbusch and Reinhold Neibuhr.

The fifth Great Awakening should make us wary of the sin of national hubris---being large and powerful is no reason to despair---between a position of positionless relativity and absolutism there is a vast area of choices for the hegemonic Americans---smaller cars and houses are a choice, a smaller military is a choice, money used to help Mexico build family planning clinics is a choice, building the levees higher is a choice, free-education is a choice. Welcome to the fifth Great Awakening.

John Fielden

COMPARATIVE RELIGIONS--ONLY
PROTESTANTS ARE WORTH COMPARING

1. Jonathan Edward's in the 17ᵗʰ century enlightenment, as a new-light theologian, protested how the Indians were treated in western Massachusetts---he had been reading Locke on reasonable Christianity and the case for justice in state and church policies. He was exiled to live with the Indians---his continued protest led him to be appointed president of Princeton University. This great awakening had other bizarre side shows such as the Salem witch trials. Puritan theology was shifting towards Spinosa's new lens on nature-or-god ---this romanticism grew into the Unitarian transcendentalism of the late 18ᵗʰ century and early 19ᵗʰ century.

2. Unitarian, R. W. Emerson, promoted romantic reflections and urged the ministers at Harvard to include more of nature's blowing clover and natural relations in their sermons. Emerson's home became home for the transcendental movement---not to transcend nature but to include nature or god. He was tempted to make the transcending sound scientific (Spinosa's new lens on nature) via what he called the over-soul. The transcendentalist may have helped cause the Civil War---Thoreau refused to pay taxes to the cotton kingdom spreading into the American frontier. The American transcenders were not as focused on the cotton factory system as were the Unitarian-Methodists in England, where wage-slavery was a new dramatic reality for poor urban workers. The cotton-wage-slavery-system was on its way to New England, but Emerson was more focused on a new philosophy for the frontier nation---he left the pulpit to warn us that the frontier would bring a new emptiness and allow the machine to ride mankind.

3. The Civil War ended with one party in power and they gave the west to new rich corporations and gave the south to new rich corporations as a supply colony. The new rich corporations invited European millions to the American factory system and the third great Protestant movement, via Walter Rauchenbush and his angry Hells Fire Church in Manhattan, came into the protest. Factories for women making shirt-waist clothing burned to the ground with the workers inside---who could stop this evil of the new factory system ----In England the Protestant Churches defied Darwinist theology and passed the Ten Hours Act with Parliament's help. In the U.S. wage-slavery was more difficult as many moved to the frontier ----actually to the dry plains for free land that was hardly free----soon the railroads and droughts made the west into a nightmare for millions.

4. Reinhold Niebuhr saw a crisis in our rapid move to the urbans---jobs are not available via positive thinking. Niebuhr saw sin as univocal or from the interests that vie for power always---the Cold War brought new pressure on job seekers---anti-Communism became the Republican Party and a bread-and-circus-culture promised to distract from urban ills. The military industrial complex anguished Eisenhower---to save money he proposed more atomic security but the 'complex' was also inside the psychology of the Whitehouse---Nixon and the Dulles, along with McCarthy, wanted to 'retake' Eastern Europe. The John Birch Society saw Ike as soft on Communism. C.W. Mills saw history as chunks or publics that have a towardsness (as Heidegger) but the culture had moved to security and the republics or states were now swallowed in empire realism.

5. Post modern protest for Walter Bruggemann was becoming real politics and a new lens or perspective on the nature of being and knowing was emerging out of German and French existentialist thinking----could the Hebrew Bible be read as power politics with Richard Rorty, Thomas Khan, Jean Lyatard and Jurgen Habermas? Would scientism and the security state screw the budgets of the University and push Darwinism as economic science? Could church co-ops alter 'nature' as capitalism and create new publics

in some places like Berea Kentucky, Tucson and Austin, even within the military minded states?

6. The old theocracies in Rome, Mecca and Salt Lake are not worth review. Europe's state religions (Luther and Calvin) failed to protest anything while leaving it to the Tudors to allow lateralized sects like the Quakers, Methodists, Unitarians and Levelers to grow and enter the political wars. The French failed to join the protests north of the Alps and Joined the Ottoman Empire in a kind of meaningless independence from Rome. Only after World War Two did French existentialist thinkers enter the serious protestant world culture.

John R Fielden

THE SPIRIT-CONSCIOUS MIND FOR POST-MODERNS—HUME TO FOUCAULT----C.W. MILLS---ANSELM AND AQUINAS ON PLATO'S VALUE CREATING IMAGINATION-AN ONTOLOGY OF BEING RISKING A TAUTOLOGY AND LOGO-CENTRIC CLAIM THAT WE HAVE THE EXCEPTIONAL POWER OF THE GODS WITH OR WITHOUT THE GODS

1. Plato claims we have the power to create original values beyond the univocal or cosmic beginnings---the power is not mystical but is exceptional as the only source of value making. Within value making there are the human interests that may conflict with each other when in extreme expression---gender, class, tribe, sect and race being the interest complexities. Plato saw the cosmic univocal as the Demiurgos or the first cause of atoms and biologicals or compounds that are transatomic. Whitehead sees these interests prehending larger relations than the isolated compounds or energy monads of Leibniz. Moderns would add propositionals as the out of box or out of cave theoria of human relations. Reinhold Niebuhr saw our endless ethical crises as the balancing away from extreme interests. Some have proposed a counter logic to Darwin's survivalist logic where values long-held can alter the survivalist ethic----the co-op in such a conscious mind-hold may alter capitalism and also save capitalism from the anxious psychological side effects of endless accumulations. Churches may act as mind-holds or strategic ways to alter the effects of capitalism---this would require some attention to the mind-hold relations and this

may mean some help from a created media that speaks for Socrates and not for concentrated media corporations. Church mind-holds outside the culture cave could include the courts, energy, media ownership, and public education projects that are free for all citizens---other projects could be particular to the United States where chattel slavery has a long-hold similar to fear-itself for tribal military interests. Plato saw the long value war between military-tribal interests and reflective interests as universal and on going. This conflict became serious when the United States became a military-industrial complex---C.W. Mills noted the exceptional mix of class extremes and the military as a post-modern arena beyond old sociological data piled high in statistical correlates. Tribals focus on borders (fear itself) and some borders are real to include even the vague borders between religious caliphate areaS and defined national commons areas.

2. When the Roman caliphate or clerics center failed to unify Italy and Europe there was a slow effort to rethink the world in terms of being (ontos) and knowing (epistemology) and some rethinking beyond Florence was in monastic centers north of the Alps. We may see this effort as the renaissance of Socrates, Plato and Aristotle, involving a three stage logic or dialectic in which the middle term is negative or a challenged position to another prevailing position. Anselm claimed we can aggregate the attributes oR predicates of material thingS and focus them as political propositions---this is not unlike Plato's value making claims. Aquinas would focus on the propositions of justice in contract relations of a defined Aristotelian state---the church in Rome might take up justice as an interest that transcends the caliphate and turns justice into a middle term for the dialectic. John Crossan, ex-priest, likes to focus on justice as the way to focus knowledge and 'being' in the same sentence as a visioning process. Jesus Seminar groups (Marcus Borg etc.) want to turn the ontos of being a lover into the labyrinth or logic of being a lover----to be is to be a lover is logo-centric. and they say does not require complex middle term arguments or dialectics. Love causes love is like a Subaru is love-----Borg thinks small things and liturgies will back up the love

labyrinth. Meister Eckart, in his medieval reflections thought justice needs some actual projects to go along with feelings---some of his projects we would call labor unions. His Beghard groups would not need the approval of Rome and this got him into some trouble with the Caliphate.

3. Hegel and Marx saw the conscious ontos or being enters into the spirit of nation and class, but others had noted the clash of class with nation. Jeremiah saw the Babylonian exile to be related to class issues---there was no way to build a nation when property classes got extreme----the exiled rich might learn or they might not. Jeremiah's critical or middle term for the dialectic got him into trouble back in Judah and a group, called the Queens of Heaven, moved him back to Egypt for his safety. Class, need not become the French Revolution, but can if class is allowed to grow and entangle with tribe and property as it did for France. France was essentially isolated from the Protestant revolution that swept north of the Alps in the 16th century.

4. There are other Caliphates---Moscow and Kiev saw themselves as saving Greek Christianity along the Caucasus line and on into eastern European areas near Greece. The West never appreciated the long Russian resistance to the Baghdad Caliphates and the Ottoman empire that once threatened Vienna. Today, the American empire via NATO tries to establish a line that holds back the Russian and Islamic Caliphates. The line gets messy as Poland and the Ukraine are mixed Christian systems that have historical but not natural borders like the Caucacus Mountains.

5. In the Nazi era, various Frankfort critical thinkers or Greek dialectic thinkers became post-Marxist---they saw more than class as the crisis of being and knowing.---they include Horkheimer, Adorno, Marcuse, Benjamin, Fromm, Levinas and Habermas. In more complex dialectics, French German thinkers opened modern critical thinking as existentialism and the ways we choose a self and how to relate self to the culture cave. For Heidegger, Hannah Arendt claimed the long effort of Germany to be trans-tribal, created a culture that has long roots and anxiety about being tribal again, and so acts as if all groups with long complex rituals, like

the Hebrews, are a treat to Germany. She says German culture has causals as complex banal ordinariness that has become extreme. To break banal odinariness, the Germans may become too open to immigrants, and give up their specialness too easily.

6. Walter Bruggemann says nation building midst the tribes of ancient Israel required a strong leader like David despite his personal failings. Another strong leader may be negotiated even by Yahweh---the building of a commons is such a leap past out tribal past that requires a complex politics that post-moderns call for. In America, C.W. Mills saw the need for special publics---some more reflective and strategic in their values---this could include churches and publics as complex as Tucson, New Mexico, Austin and Boulder. Even Santa Fe with the artist-ego may add to New Mexican public mind-hold projects. Thomas Jefferson dreamed of a legacy politics where the public opinion would prevent extreme interests like corporations, Kulaks or the military from ruling. His friend James Madison was for a large commons but wary of separate republics that can act as tribes and may make slavery the law of such places

John R Fielden

POST MODERN BRUGGEMANN VERSUS HEGEMON WHITE MAN COLONISTS BORG CROSSAN WAYS TO COMPLEX CONSCIOUSNESS---JOHN'S GOSPEL BEATITUDES CULVER NELSON AND THE CALIPHATE EMPIRES AS A NATIONALISM BUT NO NATION.

1. Bruggemann risks all via Lyatard, Rorty, Habermas and Khun---the freudian self is just one of many---power leaders and legacy politics needs a complexly active citizenship. Bruggemann's jewish bible does not propose parliament made laws nor paul's dual polity way to create public policy by negotiating interests.

2. The slow emergence of ways to do the social gospel involves new language---to juxtapose requires some attention ----Jeremiah's class and land theory may be more profound than David, Moses and Abraham in the building of nations. Jeremiah resisted class extremes in any aim to build a nation. The Ten Hours Act of 1847 announced a dual polity of protestant churches and Parliament in England---it also announced the slow emergence of Tudor politics which allowed Parliamentary parties to be responsible for public policies that are not theocratic. The Tudor Parliament grew very slowly from the twelfth century via the latitudinal security made possible to churches by the English navy.

3. Kierkegaard may leap to the co-op as a way to modify competitive economics---this involves a logical paradox (presuming economics is a science) that requires long patient liturgies to focus on long goals such as the building of a variety of media outlets that are more complex than the end of the barn in Orwell's Animal Farm

version. Churches are capable of long liturgy patience in building democratic institutions. Maynard Hutchins led a search for democratic Institutions for the Ford Company in Santa Barbara. Adam Smith assumed that God would guarantee the honesty of producer corporations––that assumption is an excess claim to know the nature of economics.

4. Bill Clinton and King David triangulated policy around sexuality and some even say murder---Clinton extended it to join Republican Bob Dole in a war to remove Kosevo Province from the Russian and Serbian orbit of southeastern Europe. Dole bragged that his diaper extended his political years as a public servant. Clinton deserves an extended comparison to King David––as see later. Russia and the Greeks have held back Islamic Caliphates for centuries but the English have helped the Turks join NATO against Russia's effort to reach the warm seas which England dominated until W.W. One. See Clinton's triangulated politics and Bob Dole story later which angered Russia and looks like NATO acting like a new Roman Empire moving eastward.

5. Wesley, Abelard and Marcus Borg joined in a labyrinthine logic or tauto-ontology that has the first premise the same as the conclusion (self referenced truth claim)---they claim that love causes love and can by-pass any critical or negating activity in any three way dialectic. They claim that love is like an off-road Subaru that does the liturgies and holds the faith whatever the first premise proposes in a logo-centric way. Bruggemann thinks we can be rid of the hegemon evils by attending post-modern thinking as Lyatard, Rorty, Habermas and Khun have done in opening up the theory of knowledge (episte) and theory of being (ontology) to modern critical politics developed in citizenal free discussions on what it means to do and be beyond merely do be do be do conversations about God doing all the important doing. Rorty believes leaving God out of discourse allows actual proposed projects but he doesn't propose a project beyond reading Unle Tom's Cabin.

6. J.W. Krutch in Tucson joined Khun in doubting lab science delivers the whole truth---he claims desert animal heroic are as original as Plato claims that our minds are creatively original in creating and

testing new social values. Edward Abbey in Tucson has threatened to use the monkey-wrench to save wild rivers and desert water from tourists and endless housing. He proposed cutting down advertizing signs along iconic Highway 66. Krutch proposed a desert museum west of Tucson and Abbey would use a monkey wrench to slow the removal of coal from Black Mesa.

7. Culver Nelson started a loving center for Matthew, called Beatitudes, near his church in Phoenix----he believes John was right to abstract from all local geographies and cultures and invite the world to lunch. Inviting the whole world to lunch has a nice linguistic communal sound. A borderless ecumenism may be naïve to the point of living inside a pietistic quietism as end in itself. Nelson's leap to an eachaton may be seen as local bragging beyond his success as a master local pulpit preacher. This view may not deal well with Caliphates which are like boundless theocracies or nationalisms. Nations that start with a tax based commons and elections are not the same as Caliphates. Nationalism brings to mind Lynn Chaney and John McCain and endless war preparations with the U.S. as God's empire maker. Senior Bush flirted with this sort of universalism in terms of a new-world-order---he was careful to invite others into his war to keep Iraqi Sunnis from threatening our Sunni Saudi Oil partners. Paul Tillich favors a symbolic metaphoric borderless unity and the communality of the whole world.

8. Bruggemann's King David starts with post moderns---Rorty, Lyatard, Habermas and Khun---Lyatard says there are no narrative absolutes about nature---human nature, God nature or natures nature. Rorty says propositions start with neighbors and not with God if we take democracy seriously. Habermas says language can be mostly about nothing unless it has action propositions. Habermas is for common action but this is too do be do be do unless strikes and strike liturgies are added. Khun says science is a nice group-think that easily becomes a powerful ideology for Corporations and the military that can use it to take University budgets away from the social gospel democrats in the Humanities---thus leaving the University as a mere multiversity of job training.

9. Bruggemann backs up to the Hebrew scriptures and has Samuel instructed by Yahweh to remove a leader who is too weak to hold a unity midst surrounding tribes. Politics is too complex unless we grasp the pragmatics of language––such as the juxtapose of propositions that may not be as simple as two plus two. Some moderns include Marcus Borg, John Crossan, Cobb-Whitehead-Hartshorne, Jung, Niebuhr, Wink, Chardin, Rasmussen at Ghost Ranch. Foucault, C. W Mills and several critical thinkers retreating from Hitler in Frankfurt Germany including Horkheimer, Habermas, Marcuse, Levinas and Fromm. Marcuse was critical of the American business mantra that leaves out education and turns public education into a local culture cave.

10. Marcus Borg saw Jesus as a spirit person---this would not be a conflict with history and other profs at Oregon State U. Jesus as spirit person had captured the essence of Yahweh via myth and metaphor which can be liturgized in small things and grace or forgiveness as did Abelard, and turned into a viewpoint. Borg did not see Jesus at war with the temple elite but unhappy with ceremonial sacrifices. His friend, Bishop Spong, would minimize history, and like Paul Tillich, focus on aphor and borderless utopian ideas as a kind of apocalypse of hegemonic forces---not unlike the problem of elites in Crossan's somebodies over the nobodies. At one point Borg did favor universal health care as s social gospel position. Borg is associated with the Jesus Seminar and saw the good Paul opening up a dialogue for the masses but the bad Paul being too opposed to the Jewish law and culture. Borg's grace-love view may be turned into logo-centrism where love causes love (as a Subaru just is what it is) a self referenced tautology or labyrinth that deepens with repetition. Crossan's historical Jesus is more than Borg's spirit person---there may be a slow apocalypse of powers-that-be (those referenced by Walter Wink today). Crossan avoids positive social science lab claims and favors useful generality in social, psych and anthropology terms. In the clash of nobodies and somebodies he is like Nietzsche in avoiding systematic systems and he uses language with the

vagueness of Wittgenstein left in. He has faith in a historic Christ and not a Christ of faith only. Jesus, as a faith only, would be a Gnostic Christianity and not radically egalitarian. Borg's Jesus is a wisdom person where healing replaces purity rites. Jesus actions were not aimed at the temple but at the rituals---he was no Saul Alinsky of community organization---he saw the purity party system as hegemonic ideology in the Jewish world and a tax on peasants. Borg's progress or eschaton we may call movement politics or utopia. Borg was out to avoid Docetism that says Jesus had only a human body that ended at the cross. Does this mean that Jesus still hovers over us like a Cheshire cat, grin and all? Borg's big picture starts with the Moses story of liberation---he suggests a democratic era did exist before Kings came along to re-build the Temple. Was Jesus clashing with more than class angers and so clashing with the extreme nationalism of the Pharisees? Borg and Crossan fit roughly into altruist social theory but they lack projects as simple as animal kindness to help their view along.

11. Others are into radical ontology, which like Hartshorne for Whitehead, says bird songs have purposes that Darwin and lab science datas miss. Radical means to do and be something and not just do be do be do. J. B. Krutch in Tucson says animals do heroic survival moves, that are god-like, just as Plato's creation of new values are god-like and unique in nature beyond science lab datas that are shy of complexity outside the lab contexts. Ed Abbey, in Tucson would take a monkey-wrench to save desert rivers and animals from tourists (endless housing) who will mine the water and kill the animals

12. Reinhold Niebuhr thinks national pride builds something like a nationalism or Caliphate-like-certainty-of-theocrats and acts like an ethnocentrism but is not a nation as such. Niebuhr noted an urban crisis as the propertyless moved to American cities. Niebuhr's focus on the crisis of urban jobs and cole-war nationalism needs a project specific such as women's health centers. C.W. Mills saw the physical and psych crisis creating a bread and circus society for the half employed masses Walter Wink thinks the commons can

lose in rituals of economic injustice in racism, nationism, racism, corporatism, genderism and creedism. Bruggemann needs various Jewish projects to build a nation---projects clear of theocratic heavy liturgies and holy places.

John R Fielden

WALTER BRUGGEMANN---A PULPIT FOR MODERNS VERSUS WHITE MALE COLONISTS----HE RISKS ALL VIA RORTY, LYATARD, KHUN AND HABERMAS HE HAS YAHWEH DOING COMPLEXITY POWER POLITICS VIA DAVID AND SAMUEL--HE SEEKS SUBVERSIVE TEXTS TO COUNTER LOCAL CAVE CULTURE FOR PLATO---HE EVEN MENTIONS SAUL ALINSKY AND THE FREUDIAN SELF AS JUST ONE OF MANY---POWER LEADERS AND LEGACY POLITICS NEEDS A COMPLEXLY ACTIVE CITIZENSHIP.

1. The slow emergence of ways to turn the social gospel into law, involved new language---to juxtapose requires some attention---Jeremiah's 'class and land theory' may be more profound than David, Moses and Abraham in the building of nations. The Ten Hours Act of 1847 announced a dual polity of Protestant churches and Parliament in England----this announcement marks the slow emergence of Tudor Politics which allowed Parliamentary parties to be responsible for public policies that are not theocratic. The Tudor Parliament grew very slowly from the twelfth century via latitudianal security made possible for the churches by the British navy.

2. Getting out of the Genesis garden, Egypt, Sinai, Babylon Syria---we may pick up on Jeremiah who went with the Queens of Heaven group back to Egypt for his safety---he was under attack from exiled land groups in Babylon. Class warfare takes various geo-political forms.

3. Richard Rorty, Thomas Khun, Jean Lyatard and Jurgen Habermas along with Levianas were post-modern thinkers. The critical Frankfurts like Levinas are neo-Marxists so they are neither into class not Hegel's spirit-nation in a simple narrative way---they are 'post' even to the Hegel-Feuerback-Marx debate.

4. Richard Rorty, of the American pragmatist school, said the mirror of nature is a mere romantics Spinosan-Emerson claim to know nature or god as one to the over-soul knower. Thomas Khun says science is tempted to the spirit of group-think. Jurgen Habermas fears the most active communications in 1984 and Animal Farm may be do be be do distractions. C.W. Mills says creative imagination is not allowed in the social sciences where positive thinkers like Tallcott Parsons at Harvard think the data correlates of the lab will show large 'cosmic' moves to solve great crises such as the Industrial Revolution. Jean Lyatard thinks the most likely story narrative of science may be another science ideology like that of Comte and the super math-physicists.

5. Reinhold Niebuhr saw the univocal (single) creation had various human interests and values that count seriously when extreme utopian interests collide. He thought utopianism is a likely sin on the ages. In the urban crisis of jobs Niebuhr saw a coming post-modern crisis for the relatively propertyless masses. In this crisis C.W. Mills saw stadia games and a version of Rousseau's concern for creative distraction to a world of happy robots and a Rome-like bread and circus society. Mills saw modern stadia games aided by electronic distractions turning score boards into Comte's manufactured consent, streams of consciousness and a culture of scientificos waiting for the next gadgets. Home based capitalism may hold out some promise to market rare local products---capitalism is a busy world view.

6. Richard Nixon's Vice President, Spiro Agnew sought to stop the critics, such as Herbert Marcuse at the University of Californaia.---he would stop the nattering na-saying naybobs and preserve the positive capitalism culture as a posibob----Calvin Coolidge said we are a business society. Marcuse was inclined to invite Socrates to

the campuses. Marcuse was one of the critical Frankfurt thinkers driven out of Germany with the flags flying.

7. Jacque Derrida favored the deconstruction of Jewish iconoclasm, but in the face of his passion for deconstruction of past narratives, he wrote of the indestructibility of justice as one truth essence in Aristotle'e fourth cause which says that goal-thinking or policy-thinking is part of human being or conscious ontology that is uniquely ours along side, and perhaps other than that of the gods who have their own univocal policies and dreams. In the tradition of Job and Yahweh, Deridda held that justice must not be deconstructed even in heaven.

8. Despite 'economic science' for Adam Smith's efficient producers of things and the logo-centric thinking some will see a contradiction capitalism via purpose-driven-co-ops that may change the 'nature' of economics consequences. Some will say that a logical labyrinth in economics or religion and psychology is just tautology and self referencing circle to nowhere. White male colonialists may find David Hume would like to debate them at the local bar. Hume crossed often to Paris to debate the Philosophes who imagined that science math and making a garden was a definition of purpose. Voltaire and his actor friends disliked Rousseau for his claim that the culture arts---acting, music and dance were used by Versailles to prevent a long-over-due French Revolution. Revolution is thought occur when many are asleep and the pulpit can induce sleep---Bruggemann thinks pulpit thinking should be under negotiation.

9. Bruggemann wants a Christian-Jewish text, apart form a question of theocracy and protests of theocracy, that are half buried in Paul's division of church and state authority. Paul's dream was slow to become the English Parliament---theocracy still resists the special reality of parliamentary democracy which keeps an open dialectic between elections. Democracy may deepen patience for elections over time---a certain amount of uncertainty is useful in defining human reality. Bruggemann needs a church project to deepen democracy outside of Animal Farm and 1984---there is always the need to vary who owns the media.

DON'T IMANENTIZE OR HASTEN THE ESCHATON––VOEGELER---NIEBUHR---DEGLER THERE MAY NOT BE AN END---SCHWEITZER BUILDS A NATION IN CONGO---THE CO-OPS AND KIERKEGAARDIAN PARADOX MAY HOLD PLATONIC VALUES OVER ATOMIC FACTS IN CREATING A NEW SYNTHESIS POST-DARWIN

1. The apocalypse of Rome and capitalist extremes may be delayed for Schweitzer's 'life world' emerging in Africa. The Greek and Hebrew Diaspora to the 'west' got some come-uppance in Hegel's world spirit synthesis and Schweitzer's life-world for German tribes as Napoleon marched into Germany. Whether the spirit or human consciousness was the borning of a spirit-nation or of class-spirit need not be settled––it may be both. The Greek dialectic in three phases includes a negativity as a critical anti-thesis or doubt about the liberal ecumenical logo-centrism of Jesus Seminar (Marcus Borg etc.)---this solipsist use of words and metaphor may be ahistorical and naïve labyrinthine logics. Borg's solipsist ontology is a love liturgy to small things, and in automobile terms, is an off-roads Subaru that merely repeats the premise in the conclusion as a form or the word 'love' as a metaphoric magic.

2. A Kierkegaardian paradox may hold a Platonic value over atomic facts in creating a new synthesis. Theocracies in Rome and Islamia may deny the complexity of nation building which leaves in the negativity of middle terms in dialectical propositionals. An example of a paradox that denies Darwinian economic nature and theocratic first principles is a co-op, held as a purposeful

challenge, to the competitive spirit of capitalistic Darwinism. This challenge may be seen in Carl Degler's American History challenge to Darwinist history.

3. Kant filled in for Hegel---assuming a pragmatic dialectic requires free-will, but Hegel added spirit of nation over tribals---- Kant added 'good will' as part of our moral-ethical laws of nature or connection to God and the cosmos. Spinosa claimed to 'see' God in his romance of God or Nature---Emerson said the way to god is the over-soul which is the equivalent of Spinosa new micro lens on nature. Kant's mind concepts were from God and transcend science lab data as does free will. An older Kant thought democracy might create practical Greek dialectical values, like peace between democratic republics.

4. John Locke and Jefferson (also Anselm and Plato) added contract rights as central to the dialectic and therefore reasonable to Christians---Jesus, Paul and Augustine proposed a reasonable dynamic dual-polity which we may call democracy. Reasonable and a' priori may merely be the claim that human creation of values is an aspect of reality. David Hume kept the English islands from being a simple reduction to Darwinist survivalist truth---the spirit that he proposed was mostly preserved in a conversation with neighbors at the local bar.

5. Spinosas' god or nature, in Japanese Shinto and Buddhist-Confucian, thinking is towards a synthesis or mind-walk of the spirit that challenges Darwinist producer economics of Adam Smith. Smith, has God prevent monopolistic tricks by capitalist entrepreneurs. Bishop Berkeley proposed some general doubt about what the senses can perceive---doubts are now done by physicists at the local bar, concerning the limits of human perception of sub-atom quanta.

6. Over the Alps, Luther, Calvin and the Tudors drifted to Roman theocracy in their drives for national empires. The Tudors, behind the north sea and navy, drifted to a radical Protestantism of grace and Abelardian love, not unlike that of Augustine's dream of two cities---one of god and one of man. Tudor grace allowed a synthesis of state and church in the Ten Hours Act of Parliament

in 1847---an act that gave rights to workers in the new factory systems or Industrial Revolution of the Yorkshires and Lancashires. Tudor latitudinarianism allowed Quakers, Methodists, Levelers and Unitarians to create the free democratic society in partnership with a new reality of Parliament which ruled England between general elections.

7. Calvinist and the English states, drifted to colonial empire building in a long naval and colonialist war versus Spain-Rome and the Habsburgs. English democracy faded midst their colonialist empire of the 19th century. Catholic theocracy kept to the abuse of women even as Rome faded into a tired Caliphate for clerics and a tourist draw for the city. Thomas Hobbes proposed property rights as natural rights but later English thinkers have proposed something called 'opportunity rights' for the propertyless. Opportunity rights gets us back into Greek dialectics and complexly conscious polity.

8. American history suggests a unity that is not based on Jewish and Islamic holy places, nor on oil owned by corporate empires centered in Houston. C.W. Mills and Niebuhr have argued against holy places and corporate empires. Niebuhr and Mills argue that Locke's reasonable synthesis has no end---we call it democracy. Carl Degler argues there is no holy or ultimate place---just this place and this time for America.

John R Fielden

ROMAN AND AMERICAN EMPIRES----UNITY ISSUES

1. Rome's hard move from Republic to Empire---involves liturgies
    and theories of unity. Rome was at war with Carthage over the sea
    and southern Italy and was slowly into a class war over new lands
    as soldiers sought Roman citizenship privileges. Constantine and
    Augustine had theories of unity that we call Christian---both of
    them were tempted to a harsh Zoroastrian dualism (Manichean). A
    defeated Carthage had entertained Manicheanism as a Gnosticism
    or claim to know---it was a version of Zoroastrianism that was
    not true to Zoroaster's actual claims to know from Ahura Mazda
    and the new light that he revealed. Zoroastrians were driven from
    Persia and exist mostly today in large Indian cities. In Iran today
    they light fires on special days to remember who they are.

2. Constantine's unity view was pragmatic, involving new Christians
    who were inclined to feed the poor-----add circus to the food
    and the new city had a chance for a peace of sorts. Augustine,
    from Carthage, gave up on Manichean world denial, to become
    a Bishop of Rome--he gave up on sex to please his mother and
    joined the new way to unify Rome within the Christian Church.
    His denial of sex for a position as Bishop had impressed Catholics-
    --giving up sex is dramatic but not as moving as Paul's dual polity
    of giving up his life for a new church and state polity. Augustine's
    dual polity (state and church) was dangerous stuff for Jesus, Paul
    and Socrates, but the state was not really challenged by Augustine's
    grace and inwardness theology----except to find ways to moderate
    German tribal invasions each year when the Rhine froze over-
    --the tribals came south. For one thousand years Rome fiddled
    with power and alliances joining Imperial agricultural lords and

Habsburg dynasties, before the Roman Pope tried to assert the great unity of Christendom. This move by Rome started the Protestant Revolution across the Alps and into England.

3. Zoroaster's actual claims were pragmatic legacy judgments of official behavior at what he called the Chinvat Bridge of the Decider---the actual public would decide, but it required a better media and education than Persia had---we are not sure America has the right popular education to run the legacy bridge for a greater unity.

4. Athenian unity was always in crisis---Plato went three times to Sicily-Syracuse to help a Greek leader (Dionysus) get the way to run a democracy by Apollo's rational way of respecting the vote. Pericles tried other ways, including culture sharing, to pull a military alliance for Athens---the Delian League was a hard sell for Pericles the great orator statesman but he could not pull it off----Athens is a tight squeeze for space and agriculture---Syracuse and Florence had to wait for another Greek republic to be born.

5. Rome's Caesar was wise enough to take France and England up to the Scottish hills and return while ignoring Germany. Rome was not ready to be an empire---Cicero and Nero admired the Greeks but Stoic and Epicurean psychology enveloped the Roman world after Alexander---we call it Hellenist culture and a vague universalism we call Platonism served as a great oneness. Platonism held the cosmos as an aspect of God's body. Rome did need other ways to claim empire---they had public republicans---those who would bring back the republic and the complexity of Senate and a second public body as a sort of internal unity with minor tensions left in. Nero felt threatened by the grand claims of Stoics like Seneca who saw death as good---so Nero had him kill himself. Cicero had no property, but in a second marriage he acquired property of a dead soldier. Cocero was an honest provincial governor but could not stay away from big speeches in Rome---his clever speeches got his killed. Cato was for individualism that had little danger to the state---we call it libertarianism in America. Rome avoided war with the Scott and German tribes but Trajan marched one thousand times into the lower Carpathian-Translavanian Alps of

Romania to bring back gold that he would use to add glamour to the city that was not an empire. Hadrian's wall gave Rome a clear definition beyond the Scottish tribes. Little did Trajan know that Woody Allen would come to make his movie in the complex city in our time.

6. The American empire was as precarious as Rome's---the confederate states claimed the right to separate republics---Justice Marshall, and later Judge Tawney, declared the U.S. Constitution subject to a Supreme Courts judgment of any law passed by the United States. Marshall's Court was designed to keep Jefferson from any executive powers. The Supreme Court has had many moves---in the late 19th century Darwinist economics supported an ideology of free enterprise---unchallenged until FDR in 1932. Jefferson and Jackson moved the U.S. westward without permission of Congress. Teddy Roosevelt's new-nationalism and Wilson's new-freedom (libertarianism) acted as ways to unify the state in continuous expansion---over Spain's and England's faltering empires.

7. FDR, as our Cicero, tried to take on the Supreme Court and the Russian empire that survived and re-emerged after Wars One and Two. Harry Truman took on the Russians, and deepened the Cold War with Russia over how to end World-War Two. Reinhold Niebuhr and C. Wright Mills tried to stop the empire ideologies that the Truman years promoted. Mill's new sociology was a close study of how the military-industrial-complex had integrated class and military families in a virtual new politics---a complex that Eisenhower found bewildering as he, sweet Mennonite and General, had not followed.

8. The Democrats, like John Kennedy, tried a milder world policy via young Americans joining the Peace-Corps building dams and out-houses for poor nations. The Soviet Russians built the Aswan Dam for Egypt as a way to penetrate Africa in the Cold-WAR. The psychic aspects of the cold-war grew and John Kennedy's Ivy League State Department (legacy Harvards) lost out to LBJ who would create the Great Society at home to counter the Soviets. LBJ had his own response to the military industrial complex---World War Two had split the Texas Hill Country over the war---the

German population of the Hill Country was the Home of Pacific War hero Admiral Nemitz. LBJ continued Kennedy policies and added his own concerns for a great society that would include the Mexican poor of the Texas Hill Country as well as the Nemitz Germans---he could unify the Mexicans, Germans and everyone except Barry Goldwater in the Great Society. Unifying Texas was not a way to world peace and LBJ fell deeper into the military-industrial-complex that had baffled Eisenhower and Kennedy. Nixon and Reagan lived off the cold war tensions in building the Republican Party---they also build on Goldwater's insight that the racist-south was angry at the New Deal ---all those rights extended to minorities could be a revival for Republicans.

9. Today, we have a new Republican foreign policy---the Kissenger-Nixons did what they called 'reality politics' while announcing the Russian and Chinese empires as threats to our empire. John McCain and Lindsey Graham, both from libertarian racist-states where individuals claim states rights helps us recall John Calhoun, who called for a new America where states have absolute rights. American corporations and the military industrial complex have found new homes in Arizona and South Carolina.

10. Empires struggle for unity because they have never built a commons---Rome was always falling and desperate to make the city into an empire--—a city without a port and only the City of God represented----partly by churches and monks who were out to soften the trans-alps tribes that Caesar did not dare take on. Cicero got himself killed trying to be a civic nation builder and Greek Renaissance man----as another Periclean great orator. The Hellenist Stoics, like Seneca, were not going to return the Greeks to the center of Roman culture.

11. F.D.R. sought legacy politics---he sought a set of New-Deals that can be changed, but probably not ended, even in a cold war. The military-industrials and racists owned much of the media and the Supreme Court gradually moved back to Darwinian economics and called it 'the law'. The legacy politics of Zoroaster and the democrats assumes a wide public media but the cold- war, old racist slave states, and Fox News plus the military industrial complex

makes 1984 and Animal Farm readable news. Moses knew better than turn the Egyptian tribals over to Ten Commands from a mountain to create a new state––the tribals did need time and new-deals considered, before invading Canaan.

12. The Bush Ivy frat boys, with West Texas crude oil having been spent in War Two, moved into the Odessa and Midland Texas crude oil fields and added Houston's great oil drillers. The Bushes sought to secure our oil in Saudi Arabia by controlling the other oilers in Iraq. Iraq was a crude unity made up by the faltering English empire that had crudely unified a place called Iraq. ----leaving one group of Sunnis to rule a majority of Shia under the language tricks of Saddam as chief of the Baathist Party. Bush One belonged to a mysterious group called New-World-Order ----this made him cautious about remaking the world American style so he stopped at the Iraq border after destroying Saddam's army in Kuwait--- unfortunately Bush One allowed Saddam to beat up the Shia as they had no air protection south of Baghdad. Saddam still had their oil and turned the great rivers into a flood plain against the Shia. Bush Two avoided the mistake of a legacy politics and assumed he had an order from God at the Methodist Church in Midland to invade Iraq----he said he was the Decider ---a language right out or Zoroastrian texts that he had barely read at Harvard.

13. Building a nations commons has been a long history---Abraham tried, the Greeks tried, Moses tried, the Hebrew Judges tried, Rome tried, the Europeans north of the Alps have tried, the U.S has tried despite suspicion that the United part is mostly language.

John R Fielden

WALTER BENJAMIN––1892-1940––FRANKFORT CRITICAL GROUP THINKER

1. Consciousness raising includes the middle and critical term in dialectic thinking---Marx and Hegel were into nationism and classism but Benjamin was out to expand truth via aesthetic theory ---this may be seen as esoteric, but Hegel's history as unbroken causal flows may also be seen as mystical and esoteric. Benjamin's manuscripts were recovered at the Spanish French border in 1940 after he committed suicide there rather than return to Germany. Hannah Arendt recovered this material. Her view of Germany and the Jewish world view later. Clearly Marx did not deal well with gender, race and sect as part of any conscious human spirit.

2. Benjamin kept Kant's Copernican reversals and said human concepts turn away from nature unless our experience is seen to be as real as the material world. Science tends to reduction of the real to numbers and art tends to connectedness and transcends atomic (2 plus 2 thinking), The spirit or geist goes beyond the sensible and even rational as the rational (see Leibniz) is never free from the stray facts---reality is empty if stray facts are left out. The absolute or univocal reality of Leibniz' thinking still faced facts, like the Lisbon earthquake, in the best of all worlds created by God. Small 'r' reason Locke called reasonable in the sufficiency test---Lisbon happens in even god's best capital R. creation---the best possible world is ours and it is partly a mess. Sufficiency brings in the connection variables. Benjamin would salvage the culture of the past via a semantic materialism that would keep the shards

of culture---as a neo-Marxist he challenged Marx's claim that capitalism is natural or the sum of nature.

3. History may be in broken phenomenal surprises or flows. Hannah Arendt's professor, Martin Heidegger, claimed we are towards complex choices (not clear math answers) which includes anxieties, fears and projects. J.P. Sartre added 'projects' so that we may not always be short of actual entities (Whiteheads actual entities) in our abstractions. Actual entities may include Lockean parliaments with a national commons, C. W. Mills' publics and Republics such as U.S. states—anthropologists add cults and tribals.

4. Neo-Marxists, like Benjamin, were labeled mystical towards nature but changing capitalism may still be possible if capitalism is not simply natural. In the English midlands (1800-1900) the Industrial Revolution involved creating unions and laws limiting labor practices in the mills (1847 the Ten Hours Act)---these efforts were aspects of the new deals that protesting churches and parliament agreed too. When capitalism or free enterprise is called God's univocal plan, others say this is just science jargon and capitalism can exist in different and limited ways or have a new nature such as the strategic mind-holds or value-holds that churches may provide in any long run of politics.

5. Heidegger's towardness, in modern and post modern language, is to choose not just a self but a self in society---Sartre called for being for others and being for self and these are not being as a univocal self but of human selves. Sartre wanted projects to mark the actual choices we make. The Ten Hours Act included schools in the new cotton factories of the Yorkshires in 19th century England. An authentic deciding self needs to stop the flow of history per Hegel and Marx and widen the prehensions as Whitehead called widening the imagination. Ed. Husserl, Merleau Ponty and Paul Ricoeur worked on ways to focus history on new ends or projects and values and not final eschatons. Had Kierkegaard lived later he could have used his third leap past aesthetic and moral thinking to the mind-hold potential of the churches, where co-ops via paradox, can both change capitalism and save it. In the edge of the French Alps Paul Ricoeur created a new semantic public within France

of motive-intent. He historicizes values or does new horizons of values---here see Robert Solomon on the existentials. For Ricoeur, consciousness constitutes itself as moral consciousness via its moral habitus used to revaluate values---this view is part of Husserl's phenom-self or being.

6. The phenom self for C.W. Mills and Reinhold Niebuhr is one that makes choices---born with a simple hammer---perhaps in new publics or cultures that are not mainstream at any given moment. Tucson. Austin and Berea are publics within republics. Publics exist within nations and cultures. Cultures are long building and German tribes were almost forever trying to find Hegel's spirit leap to nation. German geography is part of the problem, but only part----the Jewish Great Diaspora led them to this green spot north of the Alps. Hannah Arendt is German or she is Jewish or she is both---she said culture explains Germany ---its long road to banal ordinariness as a nation makes it dangerous for tight and long lived 'other cultures' and groups to be German. Arendt thought she could be both, and would let the world in on the complexity of the German geist or leap to being a nation or spirit of high unity.

7. U.S. publics are not the same as republics----republics are claims to sovereignty outside a nations commons---the U.S. frontier allowed diverse republics to claim to be Gods special creations. Ordinariness may get attached to empire as the great expanse of the U.S. has now claimed 'American peace' as Rome once claimed for itself. German and American ordinariness or culture may change over time---the churches with their long-hold-mental-strategies may help. Germany is now into sun and wind power over coal and oil, and the European Union, as the great geist-spirit moves on.

8. The banal ordinariness of German culture is seen by Hannah Arendt as the long flow of German history against powerful tribalism, and as such, was a dangerous place for the Jewish Great Diaspora that had its own great dramatic history and ego. Toleration and ecumenticity are part of the new Germany---some say they may over do it. Arendt wants to be both Jewish and

German. Tolerating U.S. Republics within the nation was part of Madison's concern that the republics might choose to be racist for extreme interests. Even after race was declared illegal, the republic treated race as their peculiar right.

John R. Fielden

MIND WALK ---SPIRITUAL FORMATION---HEGEL TO FEUERBACK---GERMAN WORKER COUNCILS---NEW HARMONY IN TENNESSEE AND IRAN 'DEALS'---ELEVENTRH CENTURY MONKS IN GRENOBLE--ECKART IN COLOGNE-- ACTUAL VORERS IN THE YORKSHIRES---EPISTE WARS BACK TO THE GREEKS---ABELARD, ANSELM, AQUINAS, OCKHAM---SOLIPSIST LOGIC PREMISES AND THE LABYRINTH OF LOVE IS A SUBARU--FRANCE WANTS THE POPE IN AVIGNON FOR CLOSE OBSERVANCE-CAROLINGIANS CREATE A FIRST CHRISTIAN NATION

1. War hawks in U.S. senate---McCain and Graham---see endless oil wars--the old slave states have a view--is Arizona now Aribama? The spirit moves---Hegel noted Napoleon's troops marching past his study---the spirit of nation or class before him. Feuerback and Marx said the new spirit or consciouness was of class---why not a synthesis of both? Senator Corker of Tennessee faces the new complexity of compromise as German auto plants in Chatanooga use 'work councils' as labor unions---Corker is puzzled by the new complexity---can Oboma make a deal with Iran's Caliphate clerics short of war? Are hints of democracy in Iran part of the memory bank of Zoroaster who suggested a legacy politics of judgment at the Chinvat Bridge for all state actors and power-brokers. Was Hegel's world spirit answering for a long German spirit or nation versus the tribals or was it, as Marx says, the crisis of class when rural folks work in factories?

2. Rome tried to moderate the tribes north of the Alps, by monks in monastic centers hoping psychic piety might meditate away all but essentials for the quiet life, One meditation center was at Grenoble in France in 1054. Augustine was for a grace theology to fill in until the City of God and City of Man could be 'one'. Augustine's dream came close to reality in only in 1500, but the City of Man resisted Roman Church taxes and the Protestant Revolution was under way. There were other signs of nation-building in France under the Carolingians who drove the Islamics from western France in the 8th century and notified the Pope that Charlemagne was Emperor on Christmas day 800 AD. in Rome.

3. Class, as the new human spirit, may be the old spirit that our ancestors noted in saying the spirit is in everyone, but tribals noted that the personal spirit could also evil and tribal war has been the long history of humankind. Hegel saw the new spirit of nation coming up the street with Napoleon and the French Marseille sung by all. In the 11th, 12th, 13th centuries Anselm, Abelard, Aquinas and Ockham debated the theory of knowledge and being----some said the human being or conscious ontology is a tautology or way of defining human being––Abelard would call love defines our nature (the Subaru of love is what it is as popeye the sailor said of himself––I yam what I yam)---philosophers call this logo-centrics or labyrinth logic where the conclusion and premise are the same (tauto-ontology) or a thing or reality is what it is. Ockham used his razor to cut away speculation about God's nature and turned it all into self-referencing---to Ockham himself, God was the premise and conclusion---this might quiet down critics and all could then meditate in lock step with the Pope. Abelard started with love and grace and avoided a theory of knowledge so any choir could sing it unthinkingly. Anselm and Aquinas went back to the Greeks in trying to create and test new values via the human spirit.

4. German work councils produce super class cars for Munich to Berlin super roads and no Subaru off- road cars for the Black Forest---Heidigger loved the Black Forest but was trapped

in Berlin. Senator Corkers Corker's racist Chatanooga (near Knoxville) has met German work councils in Chatanooga---jobs, jobs, Jobs. Corker is against unions and is faced with synthesis or how to live midst unions called councils. He wants to help Oboma do an atom deal with Iran but his local racist churches see any compromise with Islam will bring the end of the world---which end some prefer to living in Chatanooga. Is there a new spirit of compromise---Atlanta, south of Chatanooga, may soon be a part of a Black Democratic State of Georgia. Tennessee is caught up in new changes.

5. Two hundred fifty miles north of London, Marx's friend Engels, the Fieldens and Robert Owens were concerned about life in cotton mill towns that had replaced the sheepers and hand-loom workers on the moors above the fast moving rivers. Rich Englanders bought off or enclosed large moor lands for private estates---this excluded hunting and fishing areas from the poor. Owens extended his plans for utopian factory towns which he called 'new harmony societies'---the Fieldens followed John Locke's reasonable Christianity and sought a Ten Hours Act via Parliament (1847) that would protect workers in the mills. Marx was busy in the London Library for his 1848 manifesto in behalf or workers and a new class spirit. The Fieldens offered to serve in Parliament if workers, who could not vote, would approve a term in Parliament via mass meetings. Workers in the Fielden mills knew their cotton came via slave labor and they were out of work when General Lee lost the big battle in Pennslyvania---the Fielden's also saw the French Revolution against Versailles class system as justified. To avoid the harsh life of the mills, some women married a new life in Mormon Utah---others saw free land in the American western deserts as opportunity.

6. Unity problems in America and Europe are part of the great movie of western history. Monks and monasteries, such as the one at Grenoble France in the 11th century, might soften the German tribes and some monasteries entertained a renaissance of Greek philosophy which had come west via Venice and Florence. Gnostic Zoroastrian sects called Cathars settled in Albi southern France.

They were Manicheans dualists who had rejected the material world and were essentially monist---for them all the world belongs to deity and not the state or church. Augustine had suggested both state and church were one---the Cathar's extreme view tempted the French and the Pope in Rome to the spirit of fire---or Inquisition versus the Cathars.

7. A rebirth of Greek philosophy, after the long Roman side trip into Hellenist psychology of adjustment----Stoic and Epicurean, came to the monasteries. Aquinas brought the Greeks to Paris from Florence. Anselm, Abelard and Ockham re-stated the Greek philosophers----Anselm favored Plato's forms as aggregated values over facts that could be public policy propositions-- Abelard favored Augustine's grace and love labyrinth logic where love causes love---we may see such love as tautological (circular or self referencing) ontology that says nothing in the conclusion that is not in the premise----and so merely repeats the premise as a logo-centrism. Such logics are often stated in common sense terms like it-is-what-it-is or with Pope Eye saying I yam what I Yam. Jesus Seminar, and other recent scholasticisms, are accused of tauto-ontological self referencing to nowhere. Aquinas, spoke in Socrates terms of fair contracts, unjust prices and goal oriented public policies--Meister Eckhart in Cologne Germany favored the spirit of organizing the new towns crafters over the landed in the price wars. William of Ockham would use the razor to cut away unnecessary words from logic---like Abelard, his premise and conclusion were the same---his material causes are material causes and God causes are God causes---this disallows Greek values as causes.

8. Modern philosophers speak of process or becoming in terms of complexity consciousness (Jung, Cobb-Whitehead, Chardin and Joe Campbell) but within process may easily be what Plato called 'being-within-the-culture-cave-of-ones-birth-site. Plato knew the cave could be partly loaded with tribal problems and his trips to Italy, and his building a school, says the cave has many practical choices and goals to consider. Our cave has come with complexity---in the U.S. chattel slavery and native displacement are unfinished affairs.

John R Fielden

A.S.U. PROFESSON CARLSON DEBATES WITH HIMSELF WHETHER THE AMERICAN REVOLUTION WAS A JUST WAR OR A HOLY WAR, WITH HIS BACKGROUND IN HISTORY LACKING, WE MAY ASK IF THE DEBATE IS FAIR

1. We mumble about causes of jihad and jeremaid sermons but we may still need to know about the long history of nation building---Islamics often see nation building as Satanic for distracting from Allah. Were there wars within the American Revolution? Marxists and some Democrats think it was a bankers class revolution. We may learn to mumble about the Great Awakenings in America---Jonathan Edwards' angry God sermons may have changed when he lived among the Indians after losing his pulpit job. In time, Edwards read Locke's contract theory of government and wondered what it meant for Puritans to develop half-way covenants---this did not mean half way for Indians?

2. A hundred years after Edwards in another awaking the Romantics and Unitarians took on Calvinists sect salvation ceremonialists and spoke of 'over-soul' and spirit---some of which suggested God and Man were in the same experience of sunsets and politics---they exposed the mad-house prisons, bonded slavery and half way took on chattel slavery as the greatest evil. They played with the old Puritan language of a 'manifest destiny' and failed to help the French Revolution avoid the rise of Napoleon and a spirit-geist or new nationalism never seen before. Nationalism as a modern religion came about in stages.

3. Towards a hundred years later another jeremiad angry God spoke in Hells Kitchen New York for the masses pouring in from Europe to plow up the lands taken from the Indians. This Awakening was led by Walter Rauschenbusch who was a Baptist. He would counter the Social Darwinist Gospel and propose a Social Gospel as a mindset. The masses would need a new mindset to settle Ohio and California---it might include Labor Unions. For a Fourth Awakening we could move up to Reinhold Niebuhr and the 20ᵗʰ century. He and C.W. Mills lived to see the masses living in cities where the media and culture could look like Rome's bread and circus ---when jobs are scarce and the media and sports entertain us there is a temptation to a new jeremiad of theocratic politics. Could the Communists be Satan and pure evil found at last? In a Cold War there were hints of the apocalypse of democratic polities.

4. Which wars----Massachusett farmers burned bankers notes in Court Houses and Pennslyvanians defied Washington and Adams in the sale of whiskey. The U.S failed to help the French Revolt and left the French too dependent on Napoleon and the wild consciousness that Hegal and Marx discovered as a new world spirit---actually it was a new nationalism. Henry Clay and Andrew Jackson went to border wars with glee against the Spanish, English and French colonizers. Teddy Roosevelt would take Cuba, Columbia's Panama and the Pacific Islands to start an American colonial empire. In World War one Teddy Rossevelt and the trading states would risk war to trade in war zones---the angers of War One created War Two. World War one looks like a war by colonialists and Wilson could only say it was a war to end wars.

5. England wanted taxes to pay for opening the American frontier, tidewater farmers wanted the frontiers to fight their own wars. The U.S. Constitution was written by tribalists who claimed sovereignty except in foreign wars and claimed slaves were property.

6. China faced colonialists and even claims by the U.S. to hold our own courts in their land––this is the origin of the Chinese term 'foreign devils' that included the U.S. Japan,

7. Schweitzer was for an immediate eschaton of European colonial slavery---he brought his hospital to the Congo and sought a new

culture for the "life world'---instead of saving souls and robbing natives in the process he would give Europeans a life world-concern that is more focused than Kant's good will.

8. Crossan and Borg need more than good will and a synthesis of love and justice---he needs, as did Paul, to open the Greek dialectic and stop vague word games about justice and love. He needs to know that distributive justice can not be served by free trade which allows slave made products to displace American Labor Unions. American Unions may have problems with robots but more likely our problems are a failure to follow the complex ways that Unions are seen as too confrontive for churcher audiences. The Sunday School teachers may even need a Union. John Crossan needs lessons on synthesis and contract making in a democratic society.

9. The critical (leave in negativity in the dialectic) for German thinkers at the University in Frankfurt has been joined by C.W. Mills who sees much of U.S. social science as lacking a sense of justice and living off of lab datas that are correlated statistical studies and not the discovery of new a' priori truths.

10. Argument, as the logo-centrics in Abelard, was to assume the conclusion in the premise. If you presume love and grace solves all, then in labyrinth fashion, love will appear as the conclusion or 'synthesis' in graceland. This solipsist circular thinking is self referencing---say it over and over and it becomes true.

John R Fielden

JOHN CROSSAN---LOVE AND JUSTICE ARE LIKE A SUBARU--JUST SAY IT OVER AND OVER AND IT WILL APPEAR---VAGUELY HE HAS GOD AS HOUSEHOLDER TO MAKE IT HAPPEN---NIXON AND KEYENES WOULD CALL IT A FAMILY INCOME BASE OR NEGATIVE INCOME TAX SYNTHESIS PLAN

1. Missing is the justice contract (see John Rawls and Socrates) and the correction of unfair first position contract elements. Missing also it the Greek-German way to justice involving a dialectic of three propositionals---this means a middle term or negativity is included in the process and is kept there until a third or synthesis occurs in its own time frame. No synthesis is eternal---the New Deal has been testing a thesis of deals from 1932 to the present. Hegel would call this New-Deal-testing-time. The New Deal's propositionals are not an end and certainly not an eschaton or great and final end or Biblical fire over powers-that-be.

2. Albert Schweitzer would argue against an immenentized eschaton----he sought time to correct the evils of colonized slavery with his hospital and new "life world' premise that he would spread to respect of all life ---a German Dutch new respect for life forms. The anti-thesis for the New Deal is only an aspect of 'synthesis'. Newt Gingrich cleverly proposed a new contract with America---it turned out to be like the Subaru---or repeated love terms for free enterprise theory of economics. His source was like that of Moses on a Mountain top of commands.

3. Paul moved into Greek areas where synthesis was more complex for body and soul – they added mind, and Paul with the Greeks,

added another duality of state and church polity. Mind for Plato and Anselm later created values over atomic facts that could be tested in the dialectic. For Plato, mind is not just 'soul power' but a special and unique human power to create along side cosmic univocal forces---to create and test these values may take some special time as military security interests are always in a longer tribal mode for war and fear-itself. Reflective values involve arguments and correction of arguments over time and often without a military budget and a fearful estimate of the enemies of state.

4. Synthesis is not just a word but the condition of testing a set of propositions---i.e. can a state and church-secular mix make laws and change the laws short of war and violence? Democracy may be seen as an a' priori mind-set for a dialectic to test propositions. The New Deal is in dialectic for debate and voting and accepts term limits on the President. Crossan, leaves synthesis as just a word, as does Kant and Gingrich---so a wordiness replaces mind and proposes nothing---lacks context and thinks love as a premise produces justice.

5. Socrates, Jesus and Paul got themselves killed pushing a dual polity of state and church and it has taken much time from any distant eschaton to evolve Parliament and democracy. Kant thought his Reason-logic and good will deep in out nature could cohere the universe but at last he proposed democracy as a way to keep democratic cultures from war on each other----he saw no way to stop tribals from war as a definition of being tribal.

6. David Hume and others like Eric Voegelin have noted the difficulty of mixing emotion and math that the French Philosophes proposed -----the difficulty of doing distributive economics was clear enough to Jeremiah ---he had a sympathy for the small farmer and renters, but it got his shoved around and even to Egypt for the safety of his opinions.

ERIC VOEGELIN AND PLATO---BEING IN ACTION IS NOT ONTOLOGY AS GROUND OF BEING BUT IS A POLITICAL SYNTHESIS BASIS THAT WE CALL DEMOCRACY--A DEVINE BASIS FOR BEING IS MERELY FOR COSMIC ORIGINS---GROUND OF BEING SOUNDS TOO MUCH LIKE PAUL TILLICH--WE PREFER PLATO'S BEING AND ANSELMS AS THE ABILITY TO AGGREGATE VALUES OVER ATOMIC FACTS AND TEST THE VALUES WITH NEIGHBORS.

1. Voegelin declared philosophy and theology are incommensurate or at least not on speaking terms aimed of two disciplines. The basis of world order for Voegelin has an interaction with, or is in some synthesis with the Devine which we may call cosmic origins. Conscious ancient Greek philosophy and Moses' revelation are both needed to get at actual synthesis, but applying logic of this world as a truth 'beyond it' as the necessary formula is not necessary. Voegelin had little use for Gnostic shenanigans that would replace traditional truths and divine partnership. Greek philosophy, Christian morality and revelation by experience may hold the tide against disorder and inhumanity. A better attack on Gnosticisms' reduction of the real to physics may not be as good as our value-making for Plato.

2. Science as Comte, Hegel, Marx and Nietzsche will not create needed synthesis nor will the romanticism of Carlyle. Gnostics imply a way to salvation from alienated existence and science. Voegelin and Karl Popper reject a single ontological order. The death of Spirit via a single ontology of human consciousness left

the Germans helpless. Instead of ontology as Heidegger's being-as-such as the ground of being, we may say Plato had it right in his claim that we have originating power as does God, but not the power to end it all in an apocalypse. Voegelin would not try to force an end or imminent eschaton and so play God with some utopian schemes in our Tower of Babel.

3. God has exited from science, philosophy and dreams of social Gnostics. For Voegelin politics is not just an actual autonomy---a simple Constitution will not stop moral decay. He stressed the negativity of what does not work---religion, if too private will not help. He took Max Weber's job at the University of Munich seeking a values theory for knowers. He sought a post-modern view but found relativist conclusions about political systems lacking. Synthesis seeking is not synthesis finding---he avoided patriotic lines of typical academics but still saw England and America hopefully. He has become a near-cult- figure for conservative religious intellectuals. Reinhold Niebuhr and C.W. Mills tried to seek a synthesis in nation-building while critical of nationism---religious conservatives may resist such intellectual efforts. Karen Armstrong says holding a synthesis for nation building is not easy---conservatives, like Lynn Chaney, see no danger in nationism taught in the public schools. Germany found flag flying hard to resist.

4. We may suggest giving up systems and try democracy as a patience building way to limit the world's theocrats and scientisms. Cults are easy to come by. Turning Jesus Seminar into truthism is just a late temptation. Schweitzer did avoid an immanentizing of the eschaton---he just built a hospital and tried to develop a general life-value system---even if systems don't work well on the ground in the Congo.

5. Voegelin may want to accept Plato's workers as souls or God-like beings that create values over atomic facts. Capitalism, and some mystical claims by Adam Smith, that God favors producers over consumers, was too tempting to Calvin and the Presbyterian Elders. Plato, as soul-man for synthesis would call values making testable and our unique reality.

John R Fielden

LITURGY FOR BORG-CROSSAN---LOVE IS LIKE A SUBARU BUT HEIDEGGER SAYS IT IS LIKE PROJECT TOWARDSNESS---IT IS VERSUS MACHINES AND ATOMIC THINGS IN NEED OF SYNTHESIS--SUCH AS GENERAL WELFARE

1. There are many dualisms---gender, class, race, tribe and sect. Nation and nationism are variations of tribal concern at the world's borders. St. John visions a world without borders but this ignores the middle steps--NATO is needed and SEATO security pacts are not simply nation or nationism. Nation building can be realistic public policy democracy and not bragging about the American Empire and American Peace. Spinosa's synthetic lens---god or nature is aspirant epistemology but his new lens also gave a temptation to know beyond ordinary knowing, allowing a kind of scientism to creep in as Spinosan romantic culture---look deeply enough and Spinosans see God and Adam Smith producing things for sale and some will call it free enterprise and Capitalism. Emerson's over-soul claimed to transcend with a new mental lens not unlike Spinosan claims.

2. In Germany, Schliermacher---liberal ecumenist Christian pietist, sought a God-Conscious universal religion not unlike that of modernist Martin Marty at the University of Chicago. Richard Nixon joined Maynard Keynes for a synthesis to cure economic extreme recessions---a negative income tax for god's household family seemed wise but scared Nixon's old party---no negativity for the true believer capitalists---this probably got Nixon fired and not his petty spying on Watergate Democrats. For re-distribution

lessons read Nixon's negative income tax ---it allowed the rich to help the poor and not notice it.

3. Jesus, Paul, Socrates and state-church dualism is the radical politics of our earthlings––a balance and synthesis is always in need of balancing with more varied media to carry the dialectic to actual elections. Plato's body-mind-soul is a complex dualism with a third claim to crate values out of atomic facts---some would call this 'soul activity' in the sense that human beings are the only ones carrying on such new creations over and with the old cosmic creations. Parliament, may be seen as a special version of democracy that serves as responsible party politics which can make elective processes existential and almost personal beyond merely party-platform-efforts claims for state unity. Responsible policy was the heart of Zoroaster's legacy politics of the public decider----which he called the Chinvat Bridge of the Decider---the public decider being the last word in politics, but in an on-going world the last word can not be quite spoken.

4. Kierkegaard, had he lived longer, might join us and leap to a new consciousness of holding co-ops as ways to change consequences of capitalism and still be itself a form of capitalism. Kant's love and good-will versus bad-will is real whether revealed in science labs. Plato and Niebuhr sought the 'universal-cosmic-one' but with many interests conflicts left in, to explain sin---the military at every border is always at war and promoting a psychology of fear-itself. Plato would value a wide public awareness of this special interest and how it can make a farce out of democracy. After Alexander, the Greeks turned to the psychology of adjustment instead of democracy as Epicureans and Stoicals---they avoided Labor Unions needed to alter unjust prices.

5. Darwin's self interest is almost another interest invented by libertarians who say 'me' over and over again and hope to inherit a department store with Barry Goldwater. A Church can be more than a preachers party---preachers are insecure and front loaded with story tellings---they need to survive as pastors and conveners---at Hells Kitchen Church in New York raising hell was reasonable Christianity.

6. Wide Caliphate wars, supported by oil, tends to ignore democracy. Churches may do strategic co-ops to take on McCain's military-industrial-complex, local media and Caliphates, but McCain is himself a kind of walking Caliphate---his story true or false has had a great choir.

7. Parliament is like a third process to make democracy work and hold parties responsible---the parties are often opposed to Parliament details but that is why we have new elections. Distractive news---Fox 'News' etc. joins the sports complexes as bread and circus for modern Romes. Hume and Descartes would soften math with a synthesis of emotions and Propositions that can be reversed.

8. Heidegger's towardsness, Socrates would call thoeria of the possible. Theoria serve as a kind of laboratory of the mind playing with the possibles.

9. Churches have free-of-tax-land, or a special commons, where they can produce defense funds for lawyers, community or god-grids for sun and wind ---co-ops to scare the corps

10. Police over-sight to support the police and check on backgrounds that make police workers into misfits. Public education in prisons should start with philosophy as should and honest education on any campus---we can't test out change if minds are locked into culture. Philsophy is the only honest place in a University--all the others are into sales.

11. Sex education as Shelby Knox does it is in the context of churches that disvalue womens perspective---genderists will screw up the schools and leave screwing unscrewed.

12. Ghost Ranch communication centers allow preachers to think outside the pulpit and might complete their educations.

13. Jack London's General Strike can become a cultural activity to keep the state aware that it might become serious---it is liturgy for the sick state and free psychology. Churches are liturgy centers---to keep us God Conscious---the state and church need some consciousness activities to stay on the streets and out of jail except except when needed on the streets.

John R Fielden

JOHN CROSSAN'S JESUS IS NON-VIOLENT---EVEN IN THE TEMPLE WAS HE MERELY ANGRY ABOUT ANIMALS FOR SALE IN SACRIFICE RITUALS -- BUT WAS SPEAKING WITHOUT PERMIT VARIOUSLY VIOLENT TO THE SYSTEM

1. Paul's Jesus is unclear----Paul's dual authority claim for church and state requires a synthesis or compromise on public policy matters. ---Paul says God has a secret plan to achieve change. Democratic change over time may be quasi violent even as it helps build the cultural value of patience for elective processes. Crossan thinks there are hints of violence involved in John's borderless 'end' or eschatology, where a New Jerusalem comes down to earth in fire. Suggestive details in John's book may suggest violence over time---but Rome has been falling variously for 2000 years and only recently has the new Pope said breeding like rabbits, is not good in the war on poverty. Actual violence existed when Rome and the Jewish Puppet Pontius Pilate could set the rate of taxes and where no one had free speech rights. Minus details, Rome's singular rule came to an end in the 16th century Protestant Revolution north of the Alps, but Rome continued in a pretensive way as a tourist attraction to Italy (Vatican City) and as a power denying women's equality within the church

2. Crossan, thinks he has found the way the Bible reveals the secret way to peace-and love so that it is no longer a secret truth---so love and justice are 'one' or they are neither. Saying love over and over will not do---so what is the plan---can it be democracy with all the tensions and debates about values and interests left in? If dual

authority is not the answer, Crossan would try a third synthesizer, such as Aristotle's middling even if it suggests interest tensions over the just-price of things. Interest protests could be a wide range of violence----consumer unions, labor unions, general strikes, co-ops to restructure media ownership, church policy formations etc. Genesis may suggest that Eden can redistribute land in Jubilee years to re-level the property owners in first position contracts---but even if this is just love in action----taking land seems likely to be violent stuff. Once free enterprise has been quoted along with the Bible and Adam Smith this seems like a war zone. Calling it re-distribution will not please those who call it theft. After Eden you are likely on your own for apples---President Hoover thought apple sales would solve aspects of the Great Recession---he didn't give the source of apples.

3. Aristotle had other and more practical things to say about middling. Athens has a precarious need for boats to move the population to near by islands in the tribal wars around her---Aristotle would create a kind of middle class of boats families who would hard row the boats for security.

4. Crossan says conscience will bridge love and justice and avoid retributive sanctions---love itself, as a kind of sanction, is a central theme of the Jesus Seminar that Crossan belongs to. Love repeated, could be distractive, unless followed by some project content---even democratic 'new deals' may be seen as love propositions of sorts---with the caveat that democracy is towards justice and does not claim to be a world-truth-narrative apart from patience for more patience in elective processes. Conscience, tempts sectarians to identify behaviors that are not pietist and to unlove the habits of some neighbors and call that "love'. Some even claim tolerance operates as ecumenical love. The French Huguenots tried tolerance as policy but some say it caused the French Revolution instead. Outside of Eden, property issues pick up. John Locke thought Christian reasonableness and tolerance could work, but the courts have not worked that well for the poor. Your conscience may be a poor guide or just the psychological adjustment of your group of Stoics in the neighborhood. Meanwhile stay off our property.

5. The Hebrews decided that conscience needs help in a group signed covenant. Jeremiah thought a new covenant was needed after the property owners were exiled to Babylon for seventy years to rethink their behaviors, but 'famous returns' and all the pains remembered, may not solve the problem of a holy land---making land 'holy' makes it difficult to create a democratic nation where tribes can vote and are not merely tolerated. Jeremiah saw land and property issues involve justice and love in practical economic ways and problems. Love-babble would not be enough---psychologists and Stoics would likely charge for hearing about 'love' as their specialty. Instead of holy-land the Hebrews may want to consider themselves and others as holy-people, but even this can be ghetto-building that will irritate your neighbors greatly.

6. Asserting love and subverting it may be in the matrix of our labyrinth or logo-centrism---Hollywood has abused society with their own economic interest in love and psychological ways to be. Even the law of sanctions proposed by prophets may be tricky or mushy stuff---some prophets are into business for themselves. Bruggeman claims he is a pure prophet for God with his message of anti-materialism once out of Egypt--- he claims anti-materialism will solve the extremes of poverty and suffering. Others, like Hegel and Locke, would say this anti-materialism is mere psychology and gives the church a bad reputation along with the know-nothings of the world. Material projects may be called new-deal-projects---some work better than others. In the middle-ages north of the Alps, various thinkers proposed ways to know and value via what we may call 'realist thinking'. Anselm and Aquinas saw reality as testable propositions, and not just covenants and holy-places-talk----Abelard stayed closer to love as the cause of love---we may call that view 'grace' and in some sense 'grace' does create the grounds for serious conversations about good behaviors----even politicians may get out of jail and start over.

7. The geo-politics, between the Nile and Tigris-Euphrates, is not easy for nation-building---the tribes are already there, and creating a holy-place between them is bold stuff---there is never enough water in the desert if you go beyond sheep and herding

and neighbors may want to kill you because you think history belongs to you. History belongs to more than those with book and ceremonial complexity.

8. Albert Schweitzer and Eric Voegelin would say any eschaton or end is too early––off in Africa, Schweitzer would reject colonialism as a way to save souls while taking their minerals---he came with a piano and a hospital and added new respect of nature––in his new life-world-attitude that we may call love. Love is not just an off-road vehicle or Subaru––if we can find deeper ways to live with the animal-natural world. Europe has used Africa badly and even done it in the name of Jesus. For a daily rememberance we may repeat the warning in Voegelin's 'don't imminentize the eschaton'.

9. Paul, did risk his life, in holding meeting without Roman and Jewish permits. The church today, in the west, has the permission to propose new deals for the poor but the techtonic plates of empires ---Roman, English, Russian and American has not solved the old problem of powerful interests. The old tribal-military interests, that Plato identified as one of the deep sin-arenas, are still with us---guns for the Pentagon are never enough and the philosopher kings have been lost in their abstractions----proposing little and hiding behind degrees of kinds.

10. Paul, lived too early to adequately define slavery in its multiple editions---Constantine's unity-trinity trick has not unified us---Augustine's grace could not stop the tribes from trashing Rome every Christmas that the Rhine froze over. To create patience, Augustine and Constantine, both considered a sect of Zoroaster that had retreated from Persia to the coast across from Rome---in Carthage which became a naval war with Rome called the Punic Wars. Rome beat up Carthage, but they remained anti-Rome and a place of escape for scattered Zoroastrians, some of whom were driven from Persia into India and some into France. In France, they were the radical world-denying Cathars. These Cathars were the subject of Rome's early experience with fire––the Inquisitional fires did spread in Europe as other world denying Zoroastrian sects arrived.

11. Other tests for Crossan, could include the new land in America----our three of four great religious awakenings have elements of violence and anti-violence in any serious effort to follow the love and justice synthesis that Crossan seeks. Other synthesizers could include a check of Zoroaster's legacy-based-pragmatism in ancient Persia. The towards-ness existentialism of Heidegger was towards less faith in machines and for more intentional projects for the churches and for all of us. We need a new patience with democratic processes where even the church could enter----outside the pulpit, education in class rooms at DVD University is possible.

12. Is ontological love, like the Subaru, built into your neurons at birth---David Hume called it 'sympathy' and it is threatened by excess love of free-enterprise and Adam Smith's producer society. Hume thinks we are born with sympathies that can be lost in some cultures––Plato advised spending some time outside the 'culture cave'.

John R Fielden

JOHN CROSSAN--NICE LECTURE NO CONTENT--EX ROMAN CATHOLIC SAYS GOD IS A HOUSEHOLDER AND LOVE-JUSTICE ARE IN SYNTHEISIS OR BOTH FAIL.--LEAVING YOU WITH LOVE-BABBLE---NO CONTRACT NO JUSTICE

1. If you do justice you need democratic processes and propositions to avoid fading into the wind. Leaving it to the choir and psychology replaces actual propositions. At least Nixon and Keynes focused on family floor economics.

2. John Rawls says ethics is about unfair initial contracts. Newt Gingrich did a clever move on contract theory---he proposed a Contract for America---it was actually a contract to preach free enterprise theory (Reaganism) and attack unions in favor of slave labor products from China.

3. Crossan is weak on the justice side---he proposes something like Kant's good-will or an abstract ethics as a mind labyrinth to repeat words over and over with words replacing actual things involved in householding. Love for Crossan becomes what Subaru says their car is---it is love.

4. Unless love and justice are in the same synthesis it is neither says Crossan. Synthesis is a complex epistemology that Paul ran into in his Greek adventure---it is not just a nice word but a set of positions in a phased process---thesis--anti-thesis and synthesis where in time synthesis creates a new thesis.----we may call it as Hegel ---a dialectic---a complex conversation with time and propositional considerations. An uncritical view leaves out anti-theisis or the middle term for processive justice. Paul ran into

various complexities——body and mind mixed with something Plato would call "soul' complicating what we mean by 'mind'. State and church polity was another problem for justice---a proposition favored by both church and state groups can be synthesized in a limited time frame by Parliament---but Parliament was a long ways from a first reality. Church in the dual polity can be called secular. Hutchins at the Center for the Study of Democratic Institutions considered 'secular' as an aspect of a dual polity. There are many synthesis problems---Paul ran into the gender-interests-problem---Crossan's church ignored gender and has a long history of unjust gender politics. He could work on that bit of unjustice. Crossan needs a middle dialectic to take on the unjustice of gender in his past church ---the Mormon Church and the Islamics. The public schools are afraid of sex education and would leave the unfairness of the theocratic churches in place.

John R Fielden

FOR JOHN CROSSAN A PROJECT AND SYNTHESIS FOR THE METHODIST CHURCH------CROSSAN WOULD SYNTHESIZE LOVE AND JUSTICE AS ONE

1. Bill Clinton and Bob Dole took Kosevo from the South Slavs and angered Russia. Russia is now taking back Ukraine from Kiev and the west.

2. American public media and history lacks context of the Bill and Hillary show which may be seen as messing up the 'peace by sovereignty principle' centered in the 30 year war settlement of central Europe---1618-1648.

3. American public education is much too thin---Fox and Phoenix News makes foreign - policy a joke. Churches can do foreign policy contexts, but Karen Armstrong says nation gets easily confused with nationalism---a synthesis she sees as dangerous since the Cold War.

4. Wilson, in World War One, knew little of South East Europe and blandly said he was out to end all wars. Wilson was a progressive and progressed toward a colonial empire, a big navy and Latin America as our 'influence area' under the Monroe Doctrine which was nothing but a doctrine.

5. Love is more than a Subaru--- God is a Householder for Crossan. Synthesis building for Crossan is like a Subaru. Karen Armstrong says a synthesis of nation and nationalism is a serious danger----- thinking synthesis does not make foreign policy.

6. New York Times reporter David Brooks sees a synthesis for economic redistribution will work in a focus that produces more and trusts Adam Smith and God to keep producer corporations honest. He thinks our robots can compete with Chinese slave

labor and keep U.S. unions out of action. Brooks is with Ronald Reagan for free trade---free of U.S. unions. A synthesis of unions and redistribution of wealth is not practical for Brooks keeping his job as a reporter. Brooks is op-op-ed reporter---he seems to add objectivity and or confusion for the regular op-ed page.

7. A love and justice synthesis may be as vague as love is a Subaru. Saying God is a Householder--- seems like a Subaru---while enjoying the church state dual polity we may decide the state is just too easily fooled by the Yellow Press into a good war. The church needs work and Crossan may join in a synthesis that is not merely God talk---God, if God may doubt that free trade is all that a nation needs to be. The church may not need a formal foreign policy but needs media in the vicinity that is not another Subaru ad.

John R Fielden

MICHAEL DE MONTAIGNE ---1543-1619--- WE CAN'T DISCUSS MONTAIGNE OR ANYTHING IN AN HISTORICAL VACUUM---WHAT HE SAID AND WHAT WE SAY REQUIRES BACKING OFF INTO SOME CONTEXTUAL COMPLEXITY MONTAIGNE WAS THE SWEET HUMANIST MAYOR OF BORDEAU FRANCE.

1. Montaigne was an anthropologist thinker---he was a hyperpluralist, tolerant of other cultures ---this included cannibals who eat others, and Rome that ruled by bread and circus and killed pagans.

2. Rousseau was for a universal rule or meta-truth moderated by what he called the 'general will'---he implied a vague 'commons' as part of the meta-truth, but the vague commons was lost in deepening class politics before the French Revolution. General tolerance or Kantian respect is too vague or a mere attitudinal golden rule ethics.

3. France was not as secure as England behind her water barrier---France could not try democracy with Kings and Popes armies too close by militarily. Paris had to revolt.

4. Montaigne is upper class but more honest than most in reporting his own bodily classlessness---he farts, he screws, belches, craps and tells us about it. He was the 'liberal humanist' Mayor of Bordeau France and inherited a castle. France tried toleration acts to keep the Catholics and Huguenots from killing each other but it didn't work---it was too vague and lacked democratic processes. France did need a Parliament, and spent much of the 19th century after the Revolution, building it before getting distracted into colonialism

and World War One as did England. Colonialist wars with the Dutch, English and Germans delayed any French dedication to Parliament building. Parliament building in Germany was seriously delayed while the Lutherans and Catholics. in a babble of sects, divided Germany in the 20ᵗʰ century and made way for the Nazis and Communists to fill the vacuum.

5. Montaigne was a modern relativist and believed in situated ethics as did Richard Rorty, but Rorty did slip in a bit of apriori truth claim for democratic processes despite his talk of irony and uncertainty. The situated truth for France was that Kings and Papal armies had no water barrier to power as did England, so democracy in France or Germany was more difficult---Parliament is a slow and complex build.

6. If democracy has a foundational narrative standing or absolute metaphysical truth that is not available to science or religious revelations it is universal representative voting processes in a defined area. Rousseau's beloved Swiss canton around Geneva was too small to be a nation---it lacked a wide agricultural geography. Tolerance, as its best, is a faith in democratic processes of next regular elections and not a mere faith in honest essays about our general human weaknesses and habits.

7. In Germany, Hegel spoke of a higher unity or world-soul---something like the dreamed multiple state unity that Kant spoke of in Prussia. German unity was even more precarious than that of France----a long tribal history and the old empire drama around Austria made Germany a special case. Prussian Bismarck sought a unity that reminded some of Hegel's world soul ---a high unity of the spirit or human consciousness that requires patience for a trinity of processes---at least two political parties in a formal dialectic and a synthesis of compromises that may last some time---he called it epochs. Bismarck pulled it off by small wars with Austria and France intended to nationalize the German spirit and added a universal social welfare program to unite north and south Germany. Montaigne lived too early to see the great drama of 20ᵗʰ century Europe.

John Fielden

JESUS THE CLEVER ZEALOT FROM GALILEE AND NOT BETHLEHEM---READING THE GREEK JESUS FOR THE FIRST TIME---NIEBUHR AT GHOST RANCH NEW MEXICO RESPECTS COMPLEXITY AND THE JESUS PROJECT AT CHIMAYO A FEW MILES FROM LOS ALAMOS AND THE MISSILE RANGES

1. Jesus is not the nice Jewish boy of Borg, Crossan and Spong minus an eschaton---but is Jesus the complex ironist who confused Pontius Pilate and the Jewish establishment. Is Jesus the clever ironist of complexity consciousness, who took up Abraham's mission of creating nations out of tribes as did Kierkegaard, Heidegger, Niebuhr, Socrates, Plato and Aristotle. Creating an eschaton for peace and compromise--- we sometimes call the democratic process within democratic republics.

2. Galilee is closer to the Greek Hellene settlements and towns in the post-Alexander era. Galilee was a natural area of re-thinking the age, as was John's radical gathering across the Jordan for Jesus' baptism.

3. Nation building that is tolerant of tribal habits of dress, sexuality, food and ritual reminders, requires a mind-set able to hold 'one' over the 'many' for the sake of slow change within a peace and compromise political system that we may call democracy.

4. Nation building styles may require time and experiments. Montaigne, in the complex 16th century of France, proposed a slow compromise system of tribal tolerance which has the flavor of hyper-pluralism and relativity. In anthropology his view may have

problems with extremes such as tolerance of cannibalism. Jesus was a bit intolerant of the Roman-Jewish political system because it left the poor without a voice and lacked a way to compromise various interests of class, sect, race and gender within agreed on time-frames for making public policies.

5. When the Roman Republic was becoming a dictatorship the Greek Hellenes left the big questions of philosophy and became focused on psychological adjustment to the system to live as Stoics (simple tough living) and Epicurean pleasures of bread and circus was now part of the system. The Greeks built temples and statuary in new Greek towns---they adjusted and gave up the big questions until Athens could rise again in the Italian hills---Florence etc. They irritated the Jewish Maccabees wanted only Jewish temples built in Jerusalem after their exile and punishment for past failures to build a nation.

6. Philosophy returned in a complex way to Italy where Machiavelli and Florence resisted the Popes, Savanarola's evangels and the rich de Medici family while creating a citizens army to resist German tribes over the Alps. Galilio down the Arno River form Florence in Pisa was creating respect for measuring the relations of bodies, but Florence was into creating new political bodies and ways of complex co-operation in matters of class, race, gender, military security and sect---in short the pre-requites for a democratic republic.

7. Tribes are tempting power complexes and the early American colonies tried to have it both ways---they created a half-nation with a united military and monetary symbol system but kept sovereignty in the most vague sense as tribal governance. The early Puritans played with perfectionist language and utopian theocracy as they moved onto Indian lands

8. Perfectionism of the Puritans was revisited by Reagan in the Cold War years. Jonathan Edwards played with new light (enlightenment) and toleration of the Indian way to salvation --- he read new light in John Locke's theories of compromise and rule without a monarchy system---he had time to read philosophy and the theory of contracts and compromise while in exile with the

Indians and before he became President of Princeton University. Getting fired from his church allowed Edwards a new level

9. Descartes sought new light clarity that revisited the old conflict between minds and matter---but instead of clarity he proposed our conscious aggregation of values laden with the attributes of sensed things----we may call his view a rational synthesis where logic has a value premise that Christians call love and others may call sympathetic response to complexity in community relations. The Descartes synthesis may restate the problem that Jesus stated for Pontius Pilate---i.e. before we set policies we need to agree on who sets policy.

10. Galileo and the psychologists would adjust to physical measurements and the philosophers would mal-adjust the young to a received culture that had become a shamble of interests in the old Roman system. The purpose of life midst nation building problems can be stated as respect-for-others by Kant, but this sounds too loose and like love babble for the church choir. A great test of complex co-operation for Socrates, Plato and Aristotle was a time framed test to discover and test new human potentials in holding the ideal and material survival in some embrace or policy. The co-op may be such a test of potentials and not just a time for stoic and epicurean hedonisms. Instead of co-ops with a purpose many moderns propose psych motivation speakers to solve all problems---the theory is that we can start the young out so motivated that they will clearly be rich and secure---Jesus never thought of this new science.

11. Albert Schweitzer, read Jesus as a slow evolution, and read the Belgian rule of the African Congo as a sin of colonialism---or a supply colony for rising Dutch and Belgian traders. Instead of love-babble he built a hospital in the Congo and a general respect-for-life philosophy similar to that of Emanuel Kant ---- co-op hospitals are more complex than the Schweitzer's move to the Congo---see Amherst co-op hospital elsewhere.

12. The evolving church for Whitehead and Jung may start with Abelard, Anselm and Descartes claiming the human conscious mind can aggregate the attributes of sensed things as public policy.

One sensed thing may be the aggregation of money to help vary media ownership and encourage serious democratic policy making.

13. Kant wanted reason to synthesize matter and mind for Descartes and not leave the mind so isolated and arrogant----Kant claimed to unify it all but others see a clever dualism like that of Jesus where phenomena and noumena interact complexly is the basic respect for being human. Kant wanted to be both science and mind centered. Kant sought a synthetic a priori----synthetic is hard enough but what can we know is part of our a primitive condition that allows value-laden judgments---we can know space and time as grounds for what we experience, but can we know more? Niebuhr would say we can know that we need both state and church in a relationship----which presumes the church can do more than clean air and water----the poor need help beyond church charities

14. Niebuhr's new sin theory notes the ego and arrogance that can turn a nation back into tribal arrogance and military extremes in Los Alamos. Chimayo may teach us to conserve water on roof tops and create electricity on roof tops but there is more than conservation of water and energy---there is Albuquerque and media fascism---there is the price of water and energy---there is the failure of the churches to give sex education and family planning the money they need and a failure of the churches to help fund legal services for the many.

John Fielden

HELLFIRE NATION SERMON---GEO-POLITICS OF RELIGION FROM IGNACIOUS COLORADO TO DE BOTTON'S AGAPE CAFÉ

1. Jonathan Edward's angry God sermons, as new-light theology in Western Massachusetts, was focused on jeremiads as angry wake-ups---he thought the Puritans were losing their purity in half-way covenants with the Devil---focusing on property and money making.

2. Edwards lost his job as hellfire preacher angry with the interests--- when out of the pulpit he lived with Indians and read John Locke's philosophy books. Locke was for democracy and contract moral theory---Indians had no contracts---today they have Reservations and casinos. Edwards died on the way to accept his new post as President of Princeton University.

3. Locke, in philosophy was an empiricist, who said the senses reveal the real world---so not just the Bible is revelatory. Empirical up to a point, but limited by contract rights---liberty as negative or a positive is too vague---liberty in Arizona has been obfuscated by Goldwater and the CATO Institute to mean everything and nothing.

4. The U.S. shot away our sweet crude oil in WW 11 versus the Nazis and Japan. Now we have a deal with Saudi Sunni Islam for oil --- we protect them from Shia Islam in the deal. Tension over oil and religion reveals the actual mix of religion and politics.

5. Lockean philosophy, as contract theory, is what Socrates called justice where justice and power are not the same. A version of new-light thinking today versus John McCain may oppose his helping Israel take the Jordan River water from the 'Palestinian Indians'.

6. At Ghost Ranch New Mexico new-light theo-philosophy may replace coal and oil with roof water, roof electricity and wind power. We may decide to subsidize cheaper housing for poor agricultural areas away from the coasts---the ocean is rising on the old Puritan coast. We need hell-fire sermons on health care, co-ops and gun-buy backs. We need sermons not to critique individuals so much as for public policies. At Ghost Ranch New Mexico there have been moves to the new-light theology of Reinhold Niebuhr----Niebuhr's view of sin has not arrived in most churches.

7. Liberal Christianity today may try half-way covenants with our new creatures, the corporations. FDR hired trust-buster Thurman Arnold to bust the trusts, but Arnold had already written a book about trusts----The folklore of Capitalism ---where he said capitalism can not be regulated---corporations are new invented creatures where corporate lawyers will screw up all efforts to regulate them. Liberal Christianity, in half-way covenants with corporate capitalism, screws up the Universities and turns them into technical institutes giving out many degrees of ignorance.

8. At Arizona State University they have a religious studies department, but President Crow begs for money and one way to do it is to seek money from the Templeton think-tank Foundation. Templeton money goes variously---some to Emery University for Social Science that starts with value-laden premises and some money for soul-saving religious groups where love is said to be a topic.

9. We live in Hellfire Nation Churches that are angry about nothing ---they do hollow love sermons and join de Botton at the Agape Café. We did win the Super Bowl---drop kick me Jesus through the cotton goal post of life in Dallas.

10. U.S. wars remember our Puritan past for God and Reagan. Reagan violated U.S. law and said he was sorry--he made a deal to please Iran---he would give them money for military arms to make peace with them---the arms would then go secretly for military stuff to Nicaraguan rebels versus the Communist.

11. Thurman Arnold had no solution to the trusts beyond not trusting them---he never mentioned the churches or alternative

institutions---the New Deal solved some of our problems by spending big money on the war. As a sovereign nation we can create sovereign debt for various purposes. The war created new U.S. market allies---- we defended allies who also have corporations. Some of our allies were co-opists too. Hellfire sermons may have content or may just be love-babble. The Sermon on the Mount needs to come off the mountain to the do the Jesus thing--- distraction is tricky stuff---the Romans used the Christians to give out bread and the stadia to do circus––drop kick me past the folklore of capitalism is not easy---we may try some actual fire. Arizona has many stadia and churches but history is not much in demand here---bread for the very poor is also very thin.

12. In Ignacious, Colorado the Southern Ute tribes have gas, coal and casinos---property rights are never precisely 'just' and need re-negotiating over time---justice can be built into contracts over time. In Greece, war prisoners start as slaves and may work out of it---what is a sermon without some context? Education involves social-economic movements and geo-political moves---hellfire sermons are jeremiad wake-ups. Sermons anyone?

John Fielden

PHOENIX
COLLEGE---1920-2000--EVENTS-CHARACTERS

1. In the 1950s Phoenix became a complex of interests, the Mormons were first, then the Air-Force at Luke Field, Iowans and Kansans came west to see if the world is flat, Goldwater libertarian ideologues, the Indiana Pulliam press, Italian and German prisoners to Scottsdale.

2. At Luke Field, a sergeant claimed a Phoenix College text was too far left. This brought a debate to the College auditorium. Dean of the College, Robert Hannelly, joked that there was no evidence students read the texts, but he was worried. Hannelly was thinking of running for the U.S. Senate. He practiced speaking before the faculty but he knew Phoenix was far more complex than his Iowa past.

3. Barry Goldwater was also thinking of running for the U.S. Senate from his office in the basement of the Goldwater store. Goldwater came to the College asking Hannelly to fire Mario Zito---Zito was one of two Social Science professors. Hannelly assured Goldwater that Zito was no Communist and had worked for the U.S. Army to censor letters from Italian prisoners of war.

4. Hannelly's first job was to hold Phoenix College together and his secretary shared some of the way to pull it off and keep a balance of hires. Hannelly trusted an early hire from Hannibal Missouri, Joe Smelser, who taught drama and philosophy and joined the poker club with Hannelly. The poker club was an early unifier. Smelser was older and Hannelly sought peace in social science by hiring John Goff who had a Ph.D in history to run the social science department and settle any doubts from the

Goldwater right. Goff was a facts and research man and not a theorist---he would introduce the students to research methods. Goff would introduce history as one damn thing after another just as they taught pilots to fly one damn gadget after another at Luke Field. Other hires included J. Lee Thompson who was Mormon in background and a former business teacher. Thompson would run the general offices. A fellow Iowan, Donald Sundee, who had a personal phone number in the Pentagon, was hired into social science. Hannelly was a survivalist---Joe Smelser and the poker club helped but more than a Mark Twain type humanist was needed beyond the poker club. Who would teach at Phoenix College and what to teach? Smelser was hired in 1930. He had refused the first job offer in Kansas that required him to join the Khu Klux Klan.

5. The poker club didn't hold long enough---who would teach the new courses? Vernon Dolphin left the A.S.U. philosophy department to teach the religion courses. Dolphin would add practicality to his move and created a number of teaching-learning tables designed to better focus attention on a single surface. Dolphin invited unusual people to demonstrate various religious practices---one was Sally Rand the fan dancer from Chicago. My pony in Texas was named Sally Rand. Dolphin was an exciting teacher---he would give students electronic keys to respond to issues---something like Ross Perot proposed in a larger venue.

6. Goldwater moved to Washington where he focused on the politics of the 'new south'. Goldwater, like John Calhoun from South Carolina, claimed the U.S. Congress must allow large regional political blocs, even as a minority, to veto majority positions in Congress. Goldwater, like Calhoun, foresaw a new cultural majority based on the upper classes of the north and south. At one point Goldwater suggested cutting off the liberal eastern states and floating them off to Europe.

7. Phoenix College did adventure into a wide humanism with unusual professors like Robert Frank, Mario Zito, Wayne Edland and Joe Smelser. Hannelly moved on to manage the large Maricopa County College system. Politics of the college was more interesting

that one would guess. High theory would need to see beyond the Iowa corn fields and Goldwater politics. Anyone for a new course in world history beyond Iowa and Phoenix?

8. Fifty years ago at Phoenix College, Robert Frank taught world religions courses at the Jewish Community Center on Camelback Road. Dean Hannelly agreed reluctantly to let us try the courses at Phoenix College for credit. Huston Smith and others were teaching this material at Washington University in St. Louis Missouri. It was a stretch for a community college to try it out. Arizona State University was not ready and Phoenix College was in better shape for such an adventure. There was talk of Phoenix College being a University. A.S.U. had only one-half professor teaching philosophy at that time.

John Fielden---2012.

Printed in the United States
By Bookmasters